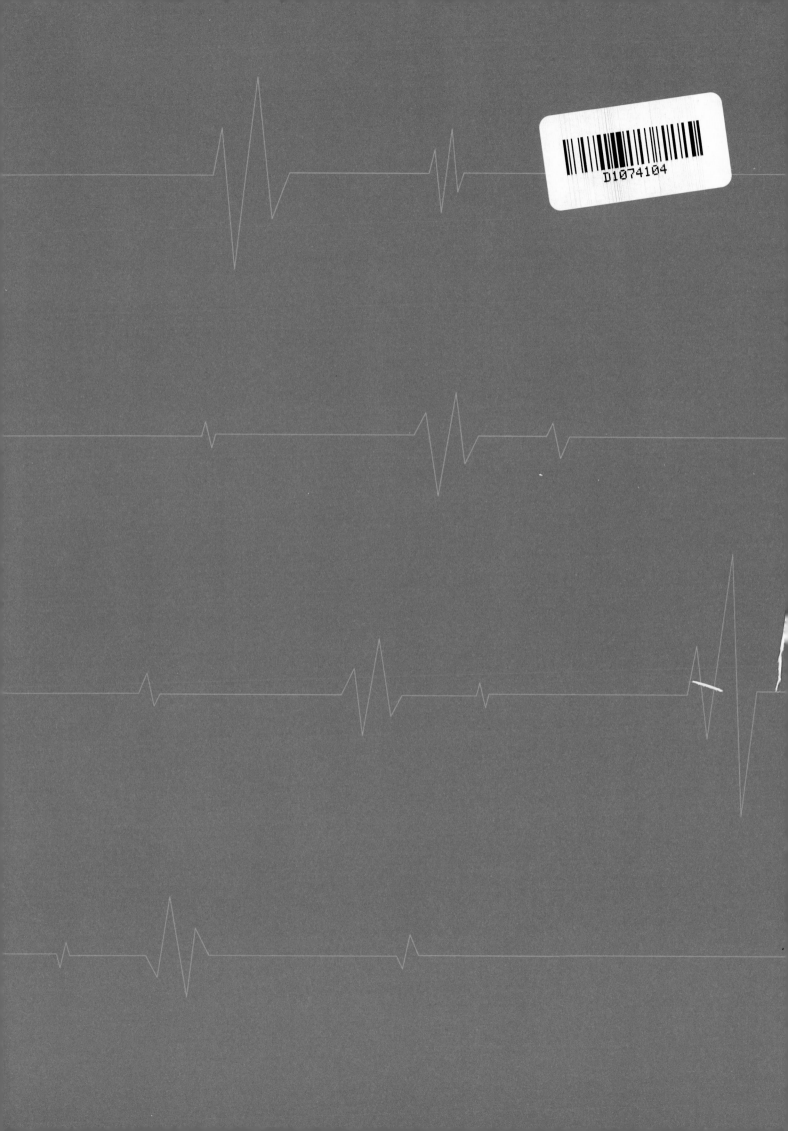

ARCHITECTURE FOR

HEALTHCARE

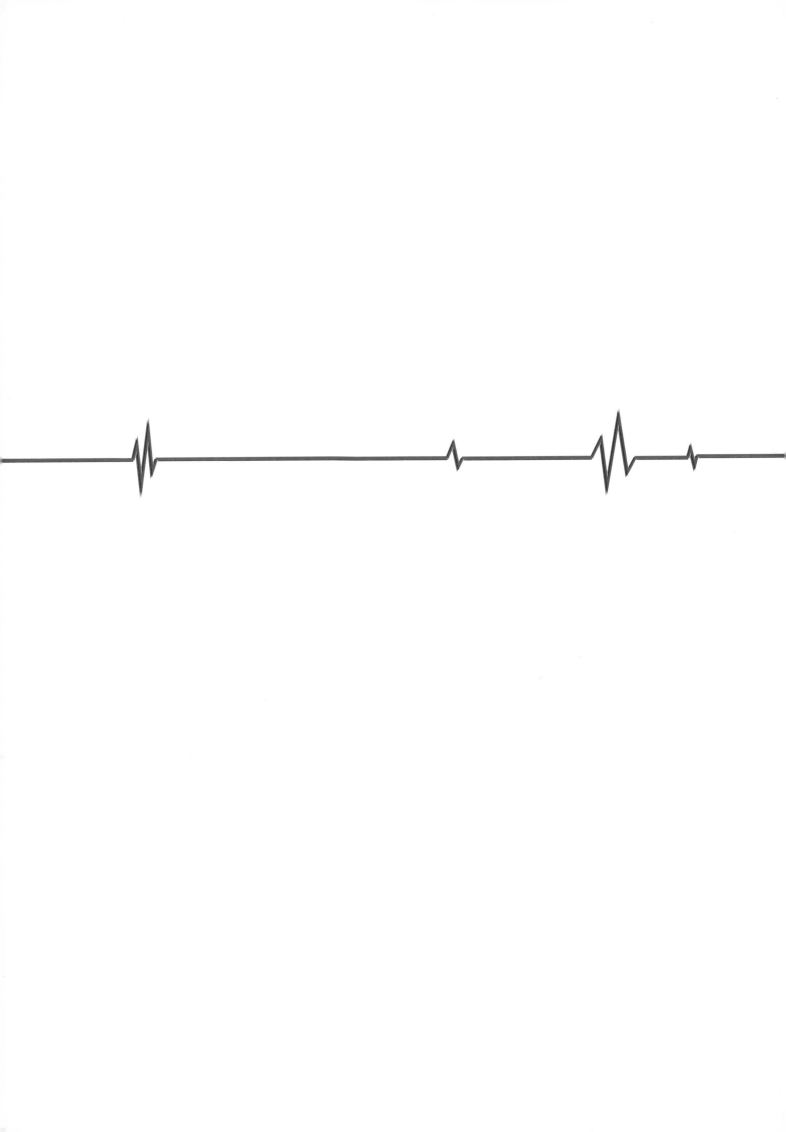

ARCHITECTURE FOR

HEALTHCARE

images
Publishing

Published in Australia in 2008 by
The Images Publishing Group Pty Ltd
ABN 89 059 734 431
6 Bastow Place, Mulgrave, Victoria 3170, Australia
Tel: +61 3 9561 5544   Fax: +61 3 9561 4860
books@imagespublishing.com
www.imagespublishing.com

Copyright © The Images Publishing Group Pty Ltd 2008
The Images Publishing Group Reference Number 724

National Library of Australia Cataloguing-in-Publication entry:

1. Health facilities - Designs and plans. 2. Public
architecture. 3. Hospital architecture. I. Boekel, Andrea.

725.5

ISBN 978 1 86470 118 0

Edited by Andrea Boekel

Designed by The Graphic Image Studio Pty Ltd. Mulgrave, Australia
www.tgis.com.au

Film by Mission Productions Limited, Hong Kong/China
Printed by Paramount Printing Company Limited Hong Kong

IMAGES has included on its website a page for special notices in relation to this and our other
publications. Please visit www.imagespublishing.com

CONTENTS

Introduction 6

Exteriors 8

Foyer and Reception Areas 66

Waiting Areas 110

Nurses' Stations and Corridors 134

Diagnostic, Surgical, and Recovery Areas 162

Patient Rooms 196

Cafeteria Facilities 212

Index 222

Acknowledgments 224

Introduction

The "public hospital" or place of care for the sick has certainly had its own evolution, being a descendant of almshouses, poorhouses, correctional facilities, and welfare centres, in many instances run by the church.

As requirements of these modest facilities have grown, regional authorities, state governments, and private companies have taken over the running of these care centers. Today, modern society demands that healthcare centers not only meet clinical requirements but also are efficient, productive, and adaptive to the latest technology. In addition, their design needs to take into consideration regulatory and compliance issues.

Attention to detail is a vital component for success in any enterprise, particularly healthcare. Design details can have an impact on the quality and value of care. Efficient and flexible design provides more comfort for patients and helps in the fight against communicable diseases. It can also increase the competitive edge by cutting overheads, improving productivity and reducing liability.

The collection of healthcare projects featured in *Architecture for Healthcare* provides an overview of some of the latest healthcare facility designs. Different types of healthcare facilities are portrayed, from large hospitals to modest clinics.

I trust that this collection of healthcare projects will be of inspiration to all concerned in this increasingly important field of architecture and design.

Andrea Boekel
Editor

EXTERIORS

1

Melinda French Gates Ambulatory Care Building
Seattle, Washington, USA
HKS Architects, Inc.

1   The large footprint is scaled down with stepped massing, roof plantings, and soft,
      curved forms facing the parking facility. The resultant space between the ambulatory
      building and garage provides pleasant outdoor space and masks the garage.

2   Floor plan

3   A stepped exterior reduces the impact with neighbours and uses low-maintenance
      precast, metal panels and low E-glass to blend with the existing facility

Photography: Ed LaCasse

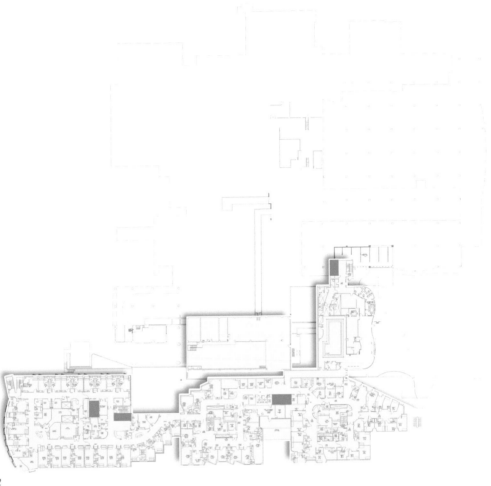

2

3

4

Encounters/Interpreters

Cardiology Clinic

Ophthalmology Clinic

Urology Clinic

Outpatient Pharmacy

HIAC

Orthopedics/ Orthotics Clinic

ED Walk-in

Ambulance Entry

Radiology

5

6

Melinda French Gates Ambulatory Care Building
Seattle, Washington, USA
HKS Architects, Inc.

4   A covered walkway leads from the garage to the ambulatory care building, providing protection from the elements while offering views to the landscape

5   Fourth floor plan

6   At dusk, interior and exterior lighting creates a dramatic and playful mood at the main entrance to the addition, promoting ease in wayfinding and reducing stress

Photography: Ed LaCasse

Beaumont Surgical Learning Center
Royal Oak, Michigan, USA
Harley Ellis Devereaux

1 First floor plan
2 Fifth floor plan
3 The addition provides 432 inpatient beds for pediatrics, neonatal intensive
 care, women's health, neuroscience, orthopedic, and cancer patients
Opposite:
 The long, well-lit glass canopy is an inviting entrance to the South Tower
Photography: Justin Maconochie

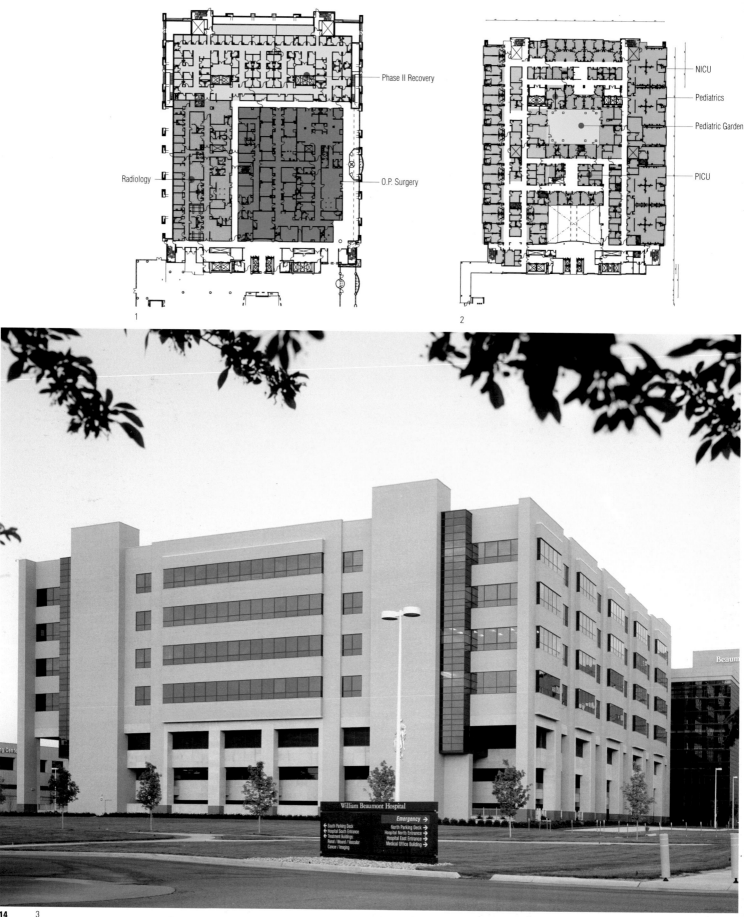

Phase II Recovery

Radiology

O.P. Surgery

NICU

Pediatrics

Pediatric Garden

PICU

1

2

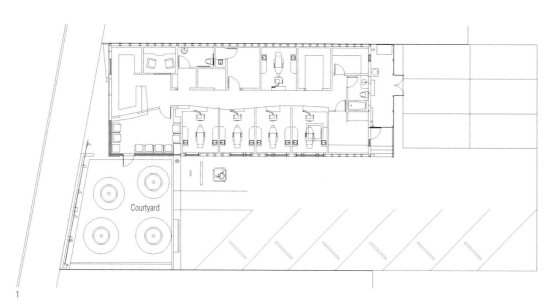

1

2

3

3

4

Millennium Dental
Sherman Oaks, California, USA
Abramson Teiger Architects

1   Floor plan
2   Entry to courtyard from street
3   Main entry is off courtyard, which serves as a tranquil outdoor garden for waiting patients
Photography: Douglas Olson Photography

Baylor Clinic
Houston, Texas, USA
Kirksey Architecture

4   This state-of-the-art, patient-friendly facility has easy access to St. Luke's Episcopal through a convenient connecting skybridge
Photography: Aker/Zvonkovic Photography

Providence Newberg Medical Center
Newberg, Oregon, USA
Mahlum Architects

1. Exterior at dusk. Clear circulation is achieved through the two-story glassed entry and galleria spine that provide a single point of entry and connects to the diverse services located around the healing gardens.
2. Floor plan. The medical center is composed of two distinct elements: a 40-bed acute care hospital and a medical office building that are organized around two healing gardens and linked by the two-story café.
3. West healing garden at dusk. Natural light fills interior spaces via the north-facing gallery/waiting areas (including the waiting room of the emergency department on the right), which overlook both gardens.
4. East healing garden. Both healing gardens provide a selection of drought-tolerant plants, which reduces irrigation demands by 50 percent creating energy-efficient savings for the medical center.

Photography: Benjamin Benschneider (1&3), Eckert & Eckert (4)

1

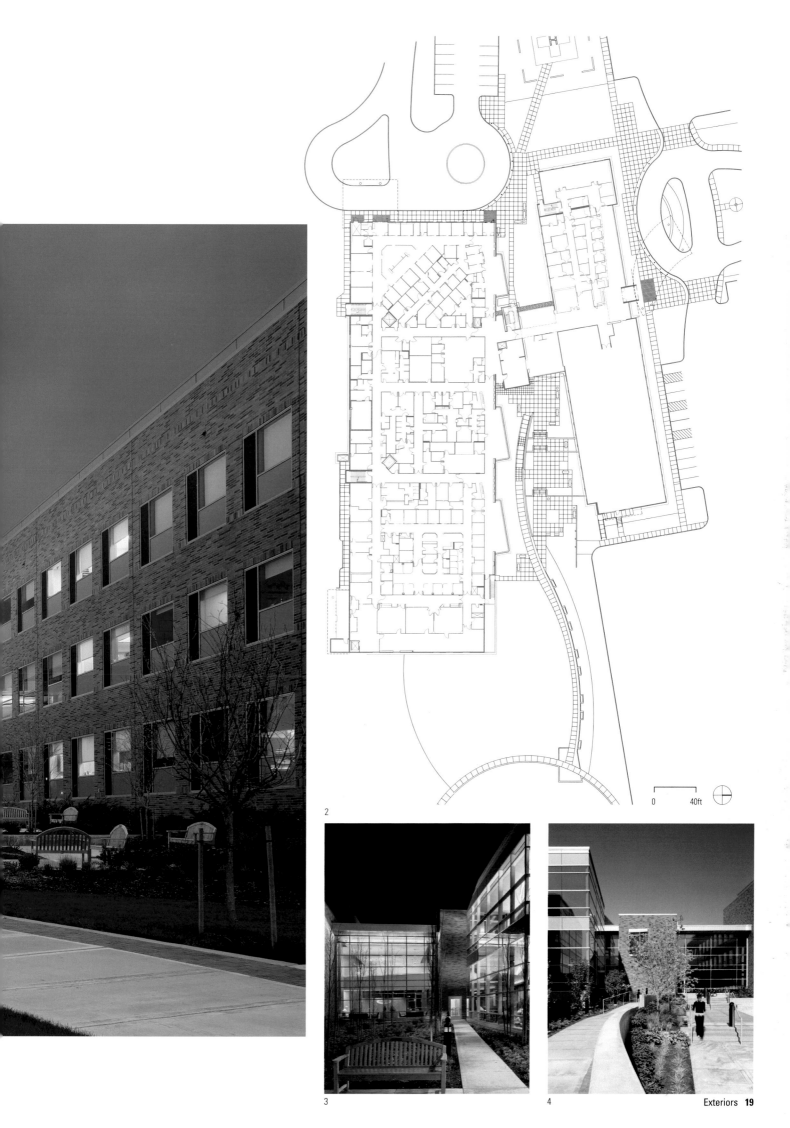

2

3 4 Exteriors **19**

Wellpointe
Rochester Hills, Michigan, USA
Harley Ellis Devereaux

1   Floor plan
2   The south façade of the Medical
    Office Building is clad in brick to
    provide a warmer, more residential
    feel to the building

Photography: Laszlo Regos

The Wisconsin Heart Hospital
Wauwatosa, Wisconsin, USA
HDR Architecture, Inc.

3   The 127,000 square-foot, two-story hospital is divided in the center by an atrium
    entrance. Lower in the middle and higher at both ends, the atrium extends the
    entire length of the building.
4   The hospital's exterior design, which features architectural precast concrete with
    a two-tone finish of smooth and heavy sandblasting, was recognized with a Civic
    Appreciation award from the West Suburban Chamber of Commerce in Wauwatosa
5   First floor plan

Photography: Mark Ballogg @ Steinkamp/Ballogg

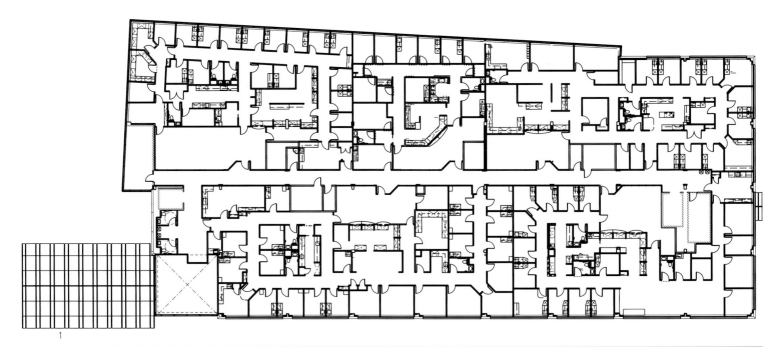

1

3

4

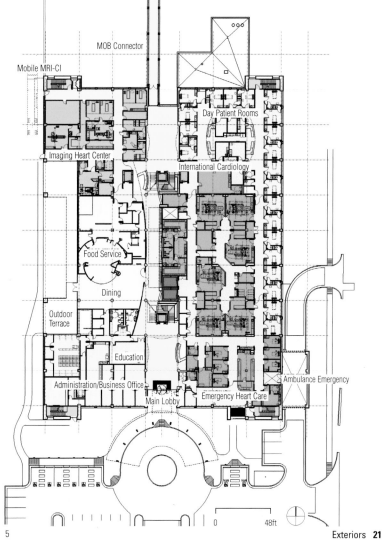

MOB Connector

Mobile MRI-CI

Day Patient Rooms

Imaging Heart Center

International Cardiology

Food Service

Dining

Outdoor
Terrace

Education

Administration/Business Office

Ambulance Emergency

Main Lobby

Emergency Heart Care

0   48ft

5

1

3

2

Abbott Northwestern Heart Hospital
Minneapolis, Minnesota, USA
HKS Architects, Inc.

1   The rhythm and scale of the west façade reflect the homes across the park
2   Heart hospital addition with rotunda connection to parking garage
3   Dramatic light enhances the main entry at night and creates a glow from
    within public waiting areas

Photography: Ed LaCasse

1

2

3

4

Washington Regional Medical Center
Fayetteville, Arkansas, USA
HKS Architects, Inc.
1&3   View of medical center at night
  2   The Women's Center has its own dedicated entrance
  4   The main entrance has a warm and inviting feel with
       walking paths and landscaped gardens
Photography: Ed LaCasse

St Rose Dominican Hospital, Siena Campus
Henderson, Nevada, USA
HKS Architects, Inc.

1&2 Main entrance sidewalk is lined with palm trees

3 Statue within xeriscape provides an air of tranquillity

4 Ball-shaped accents and details in paved areas add interest to outdoor areas

Photography: Ed LaCasse

2

3

4

1

Memorial Hermann Medical Plaza
Houston, Texas, USA
Kirksey Architecture
1   View of building from Rice University
2   First floor plan
3   Macgregor Drive entry lobby
Photography: Aker/Zvonkovic Photography

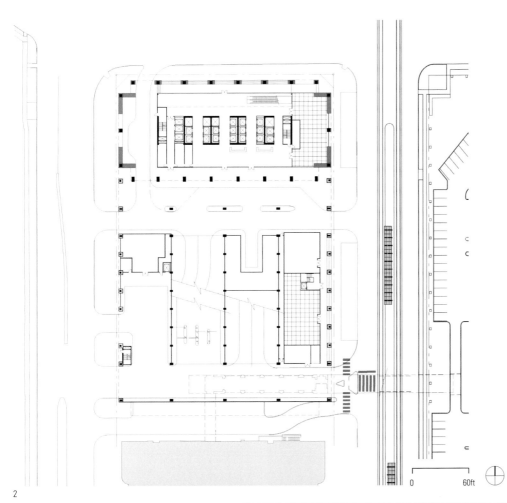

2

3

1

2

UNC Children's & Women's Hospital
Chapel Hill, North Carolina, USA
HKS Architects, Inc.
1   Children's and women's addition with two-story concourse
2   Entrance to children's hospital
Photography: Wes Thompson

1

McKay-Dee Hospital Center
Ogden, Utah, USA
HKS Architects, Inc.
1   The integration of landscaping and water features are incorporated with the building's exterior
2   Entrance is complemented by Utah sandstone entry canopy
3   Utah red sandstone used as building accent
Photography: Blake Marvin

2

3

4

5

McKay-Dee Hospital Center
Ogden, Utah, USA
HKS Architects, Inc.

4–7   The Hospital Center is a nonprofit, 317-bed full-service tertiary and acute care referral center. With 10 affiliated clinics, McKay-Dee serves northern Utah, and portions of southeast Idaho and western Wyoming. It offers nationally ranked programs such as the Heart & Vascular Institute, the Newborn ICU and a new Cancer Treatment Center. Other centers include Emergency and Level II Trauma Care, Critical Care, Women & Children's Services, Stewart Rehabilitation Center, Behavioral Medicine, and the Community Health Information Center.

Photography: Blake Marvin

6

7

1

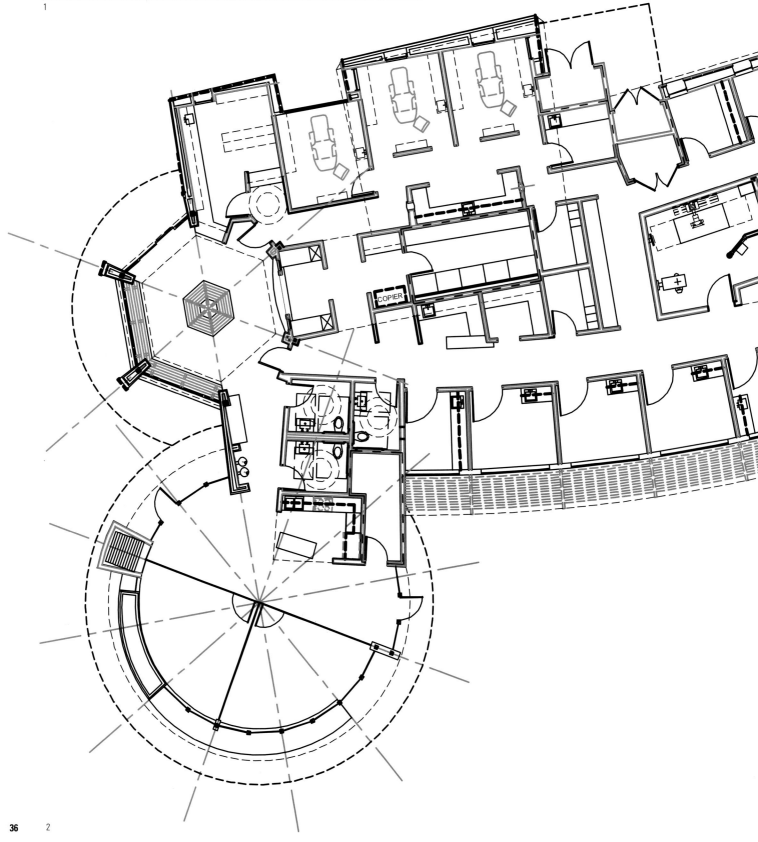

COPIER

Santa Ysabel Community Center
Santa Ysabel, California, USA
HMC Architects

1 Located on the Santa Ysabel Reservation, the center combines Native-American history, ancient culture, high design, and spirituality with state-of-the-art technology. To strengthen the link with the natural environment, an oak tree behind the facility is structurally represented in the lobby.

2 The floor plan is organized into related functional areas that promote a natural flow of circulation

Photography: Jim Brady

Renown Health South Meadows Diagnostic and Treatment Pavilion
Reno, Nevada, USA
HMC Architects

3 Regional characteristics were borrowed to create this dramatic exterior

4 The east elevation of the building features the emergency entrance on the right and the stair tower in the center

Photography: Vance Fox

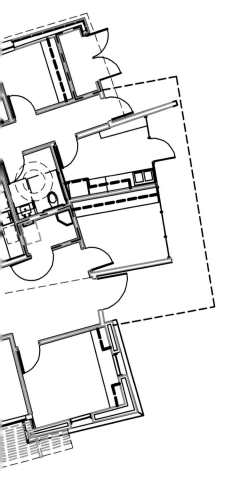

3

4

Women's
Center

↗ Patient Drop-off
Parking

Cancer Center

Clarian West Medical Center
Avon, Indiana, USA
HKS Architects Inc.
Previous pages:
    A separate women's center entry provides convenient and immediate access
    for expecting mothers
Opposite:
    Entry to Cancer Center
3   Warm brick tones in combination with stone accent the colors of the region
4   A warm palette of materials and textures provides a comfortable backdrop to
    one of many gardens found on campus
Photography: Ed LaCasse

3

4

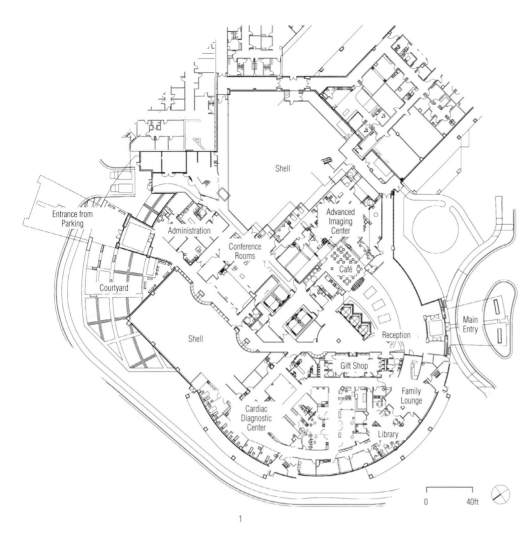

1

Sentara Heart Hospital
Norfolk, Virginia, USA
HDR Architecture, Inc.

1 Floor plan
2 The new Sentara Heart Hospital was designed as a "state-of-the-heart"
   facility allowing patients to receive all cardiac services under one roof
3 The exterior's loggia-style open base, brown granite accent walls, and
   buff-colored modular brick maintain a sensitivity to the architecture of
   the surrounding area

Photography: Mark Ballogg

2

3

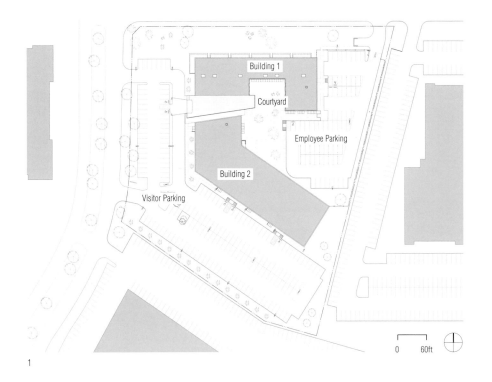

1

Building 1

Courtyard

Employee Parking

Building 2

Visitor Parking

0   60ft

2

3

Lantern Bend Medical Office Building
Houston, Texas, USA
Kirksey Architecture

   1   Floor plan
2&3   Exterior of Lantern Bend Medical
      Office Building
Photography: Aker/Zvonkovic Photography

Clarian North Medical Center
Carmel, Indiana, USA
HKS Architects, Inc.
Previous pages:
   Dedicated women's and children's
   speciality center entrance
2   Third level floor plan
3   The facility is a stately
    expression to the business
    community
4   Decorative lakes adorn the
    Clarian North campus

Photography: Jeff Millies, Hedrich
Blessing Photography

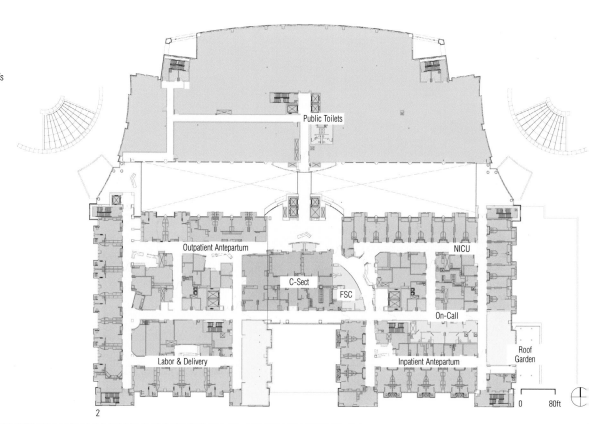

Public Toilets

Outpatient Antepartum

NICU

C-Sect

FSC

On-Call

Roof
Garden

Labor & Delivery

Inpatient Antepartum

0   80ft

2

4

Obici Hospital
Suffolk, Virginia, USA
HKS Architects, Inc.

1   Ground floor plan
2   Traditional materials such as stone and brick create a comfortable and inviting campus environment
3   The bed tower was oriented to take advantage of the views to the eastern wetlands and the subdued morning light
4   Main entry and drop-off porte-cochere emulates a lighthouse as a welcoming icon

Photography: Ed LaCasse

1

2

3

4

Parker Adventist Hospital
Parker, Colorado, USA
HKS Architects, Inc.

1 Floor-to-ceiling glass in family waiting areas provides access to natural light and views to nature
2 The main entrance is reminiscent of mountain lodges
3 Patient care units are designed to maximize views to the Front Range Mountains

Following pages:
    The dining courtyard allows visitors to enjoy an outdoor dining experience

Photography: Ed LaCasse

1

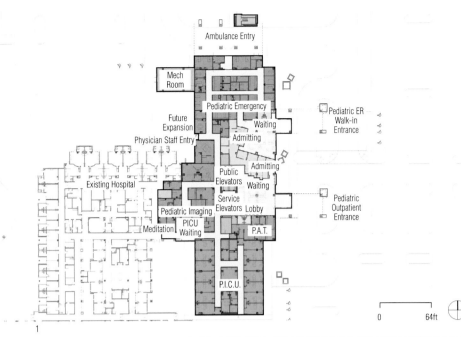

Ambulance Entry

Mech Room

Pediatric Emergency

Future Expansion

Waiting

Physician Staff Entry

Admitting

Existing Hospital

Admitting

Public Elevators

Waiting

Service Elevators

Pediatric Imaging

Lobby

Meditation

PICU Waiting

P.A.T.

P.I.C.U.

Pediatric ER Walk-in Entrance

Pediatric Outpatient Entrance

0   64ft

1

2

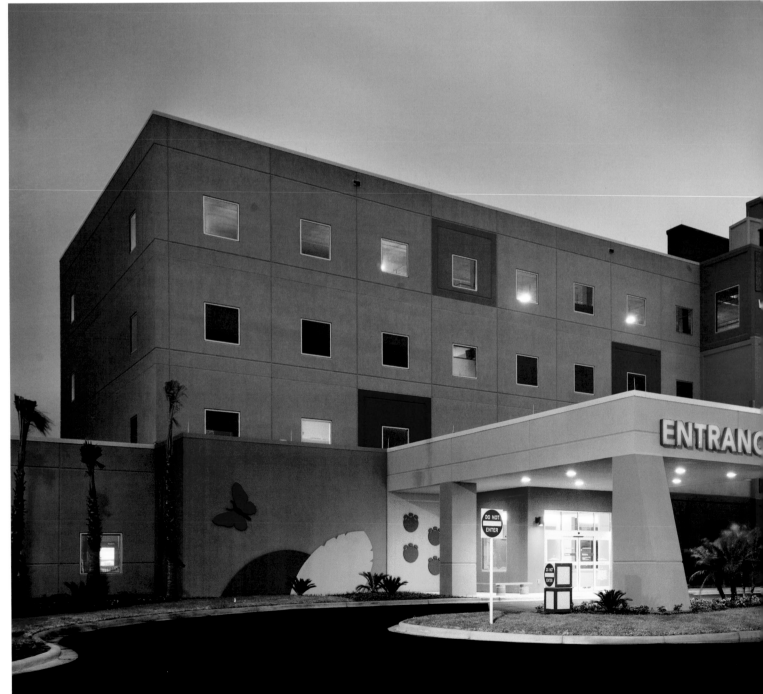

4

Edinburg Children's Hospital
Edinburg, Texas, USA
HKS Architects, Inc.

1   Floor plan
2   Standing like a giant children's toy box the Edinburg Childrens' Hospital architecture and graphics are functional yet inviting and playful
3   A child-friendly design helps reduce anxiety in children and their families
4   Bright colors, whimsical animal graphics, and bold geometric building blocks create a stimulating, dynamic environment

Photography: Ed LaCasse

1

2

Christus Muguerza del Sur
Monterrey, Mexico
HKS Architects, Inc.
1   The hospital is nestled between two branches of the Sierra Madre Mountains
2   Monterrey, the heaquarters of Christus Muguerza, is one of the leading industrial and financial centers of Mexico. The design of the hospital pays heed to the surrounding landscape.
3   A five-story, circular glass rotunda denotes the main entry
4   Curved walls screen healing spaces from vehicular traffic
Photography: Blake Marvin

5

Christus Muguerza del Sur
Monterrey, Mexico
HKS Architects, Inc.

5   Christus Muguerza del Sur's unique design sets it apart from typical buildings in Monterrey
6   Views of the spectacular mountains surrounding Monterrey are available from every window of this stunning facility, and patient recovery suites are the most comfortable and beautiful in the entire Christus Muguerza network. This world-class facility opened with 100 beds and a 120-office medical tower.
7   The colorful design and open architecture of the hospital is a special feature complementing the natural environment with green reflective glass and an earth-toned color palette

Photography: Blake Marvin

6

7

1

2

3

St. Mary's Medical Center
Duluth, Minnesota, USA
HKS Architects, Inc.
1   The building is located on a hill overlooking Lake Superior
2   The dining area and skywalk connector overlook the healing garden
3   The building, located on a redeveloped urban brownfield site, faces Duluth's main downtown street
4   The main lobby looks south over a landscaped hillside to Lake Superior beyond
Photography: Ed LaCasse

4

St. Mary's Medical Center
Duluth, Minnesota, USA
HKS Architects, Inc.

5 Therapeutic gardens are landscaped with drought-resistant native plants that do not require irrigation
6 The skywalk connector provides a covered walkway between the existing St. Mary's/Duluth Miller-Dwan Medical Center and the First Street Building
7 An outdoor dining terrace is located on the second level

Photography: Ed LaCasse

6

7

FOYER AND RECEPTION AREAS

Foster Family Atrium

**Melinda French Gates Ambulatory Care Building
Seattle, Washington, USA**
HKS Architects, Inc

Opposite:
    A curving low wall with a wavy-topped art glass panel
    further defines the outpatient waiting area. Carpeted
    to provide sound attenuation the waiting areas are a
    relaxing space

2   The pinwheel registration area is designed with
    ergonomics and privacy in mind

3   Inlaid terrazzo sea creatures lead children and parents
    to a centralized registration area for the sub-speciality
    clinics. Geometry, lighting, and colorful sea creatures
    are repeated on both clinical floors

Photography: Ed LaCasse

2

3

Melinda French Gates Ambulatory Care Building
Seattle, Washington, USA
HKS Architects, Inc.

4 The three-story atrium acts as the primary interior wayfinding element while creatively providing a waiting space for outpatients. A six-ton cast glass-and-steel whale mother and child anchors the space

5 Generous donations allowed Coast Salish artist Susan Point to create a stunning wall relief representing the circle of life, which punctuates the fourth-floor atrium entrance and provides a calming, stress-relieving accent

Photography: Ed LaCasse

5

1 Many family-friendly amenities were incorporated
into the facility that includes a multi-story lobby,
complete with a flowing river. The atrium space is
multi-functional and acts as a place for families and
staff to socialize and gather for special events.

Photography: Tom Kessler Photography

1

Children's Hospital
Omaha, Nebraska, USA
HDR Architecture, Inc.

1 Sprinkled throughout the whimsical hallways are a collection of creative paintings from patients and local artists that help lift the spirits of patients and families during their stay

Photography: Tom Kessler Photography

Abbott Northwestern Heart Hospital
Minneapolis, Minnesota, USA
HKS Architects, Inc.

2 Entrance to hospital

3 Sub-wait areas in diagnostic clinic expedite patient throughput and increase patient satisfaction

4 A fireplace creates a soothing atmosphere in the family care center

Photography: Ed LaCasse

1

2

3

4

Washington Regional Medical Center
Fayetteville, Arkansas, USA
HKS Architects, Inc.
1   Main entry waiting area
2   Atrium overlooking first floor seating area
3   Main atrium
Photography: Ed LaCasse

McKay-Dee Hospital Center
Ogden, Utah, USA
HKS Architects, Inc.
4   Reception areas provide connections on
    each floor between the hospital and the
    physicians' office environment
Photography: Blake Marvin

2

3

4

Memorial Hermann Medical Plaza
Houston, Texas, USA
Kirksey Architecture

1 Main lobby from second floor
2 Main lobby
3 Rear lobby and information desk from parking garage
Opposite:
  Main lobby from second floor
Photography: Aker/Zvonkovic Photography

1

2

3

**West Coast Radiology Center
Laguna Niguel, California, USA**
Saunders + Wiant Architects

1   Reception and patient lounge areas
Photography: Ian Wiant

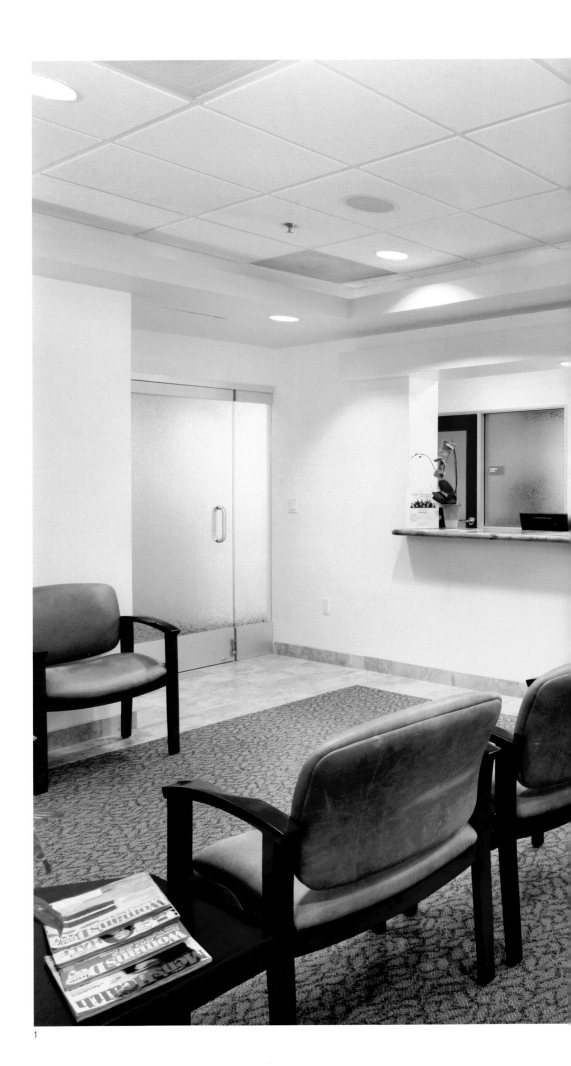

1

UNC Children's & Women's Hospital
Chapel Hill, North Carolina, USA
HKS Architects, Inc.

1 Children's hospital atrium creates positive
distractions through kinetic sculptures,
lights, and stage performances
2 Concourse link and information desk
3 Public concourse link between children
and women's lobbies
4 Lobby contains a luminous glass ceiling
that lets in plenty of light

Photography: Wes Thompson

1

2

3

4

Riverview Psychiatric Treatment Center
Augusta, Maine, USA
JSA Inc.
1   Public lobby. The combination of artificial
    and natural daylight bathes this space in
    a diffused glow.
Photography: Peter Urbanski

Christus Muguerza del Sur
Monterrey, Mexico
HKS Architects, Inc.
2   Tall bamboo plants form part of the
    interior design
Photography: Blake Marvin

2

Ladera Ranch Pediatric Dentistry
Ladera Ranch, California, USA
Saunders + Wiant Architects

Opposite:
    Check-out counter features a banyan tree
2   Counter optimises usage of space with its
    curvilinear design
Photography: Ian Wiant

Coastal Kids Children's Medical Group
Newport Beach, California, USA
Saunders + Wiant Architects

3   Primary colors and shapes that project a
    playful element feature prominently in
    the design at the reception counter
Photography: Ian Wiant

2

3

Firelands Regional Medical Center
Sandusky, Ohio, USA
Harley Ellis Devereaux
Opposite:
  Daylit atrium includes a water feature with
  live plantings to create a comfortable
  space for patients and their families
Photography: Steve Maylone Photography

Clarian North Medical Center
Carmel, Indiana, USA
HKS Architects. Inc.
2 Five symbols of sacred geometry—Tree of Life, Seed
   of Life, Flower of Life, Golden Spiral and The Circle
   are used repeatedly in artwork, lighting fixtures, wall
   tiles, flooring, fabrics, and many other design aspects
Photography: Jeff Millies, Hedrich Blessing Photography

2

1

1 Family and pediatric activity areas are provided throughout the unit for patient comfort
2 Open work areas provide visible and direct views to patient areas from the nursing units
3 Entry foyer offers patients and visitors access to both human and high-tech interaction
Photography: Ed LaCasse

2

3

1

2

3

The Wisconsin Heart Hospital
Wauwatosa, Wisconsin, USA
HDR Architecture, Inc.
1   Wide windows in family waiting areas that overlook the
    sun-filled atrium bring in abundant natural light
2   Waiting area. Many of the public spaces including the
    lobby feature interior design details that were chosen
    to make patients feel they are checking into an upscale
    hotel rather than a hospital.
Photography: Mark Ballogg

Clear Image Dental and Medical Spa
Mission Viejo, California, USA
Saunders + Wiant Architects
3   Main entrance and reception area
Photography: Ian Wiant

Sentara Heart Hospital
Norfolk, Virginia, USA
HDR Architecture, Inc.
4   The use of natural woods and warm-toned colors
    conveys a sense of peace and tranquillity
5   The lobby is the building's signature space with its open
    and airy feel dramatically opening up into two stories
Photography: Mark Ballogg

4

5

Baptist Health Medical Center
North Little Rock, Arkansas, USA
HKS Architects, Inc.

1   Natural light permeates the two-story atrium area
Photography: King Graf

Wellpointe Medical Office Building
Rochester Hills, Michigan, USA
Harley Ellis Devereaux

2   The physician-owned medical office building houses
     15 medical practices. The foyer area has a minimalist
     theme with contemporary floor tiles, lighting, and
     window accents providing style.
Photography: Laszlo Regos Photography

1

Cancer Care Center of York County
Sanford, Maine, USA
JSA Inc.

1   Lobby waiting area. Beams, arched windows, and multi-level
    lighting make for a relaxed and informal setting.
2   A cosy fireplace offers a welcoming feel while views to the
    outdoors provide a sense of calm

Photography: Blind Dog Photography

2

Lantern Bend Medical Office Building
Houston, Texas, USA
Kirksey Architects

1   Main lobby—extensive use of glass brings in plenty of daylight
2   Main lobby—subtle lighting provides a restful ambience
3   Main lobby—views to the outdoors are available through floor-to-ceiling windows
Photography: Aker/Zvonkovic Photography

2

3

1

2

Obici Hospital
Suffolk, Virginia, USA
HKS Architects, Inc.

1 Lobby rotunda serves as the main reception area and provides intuitive wayfinding
2 Aerial view of hospital reception area
3 View to main entrance from interior atrium
4 Interior atrium showcases natural light and warm colors, and provides ample public spaces for patients and their family members

Photography: Ed LaCasse (1,3&4), Brad Sindle (2)

4

1

2

Parker Adventist Hospital
Parker, Colorado, USA
HKS Architects, Inc.
1   Carpet inset into polished terrazzo flooring addresses large-scale volumes of space while creating
    human-scaled areas for intimate family waiting areas
2   Three-story fireplace anchors the spacious light-filled lobby at main entrance
3   Lobby is accented with wood, stone, and metal to emulate historic mountain retreats and healing spas
Photography: Ed LaCasse

4

↑ Emergency
↑ Pediatrics
↑ Rest Rooms
→ Radiology

6

Parker Adventist Hospital
Parker, Colorado, USA
HKS Architects, Inc.

4   Regional vocabulary of forms and materials are presented in a straightforward,
    contemporary manner to create a comfortable, human-scaled environment
5   Clear wayfinding graphics allow patients and families to easily navigate their
    way through the facility
6   Art is located throughout the facility to add a feeling of comfort as well as
    additional orienting and wayfinding cues

Photography: Ed LaCasse

1

St. Mary's Medical Center
Duluth, Minnesota, USA
HKS Architects, Inc.

1   Two-story public lobby with reception desk at center. The Cancer Center and Digestive
    Diseases Center waiting areas are on the second-level balconies.
2   Clinic waiting areas overlook the main lobby and panoramic views of Lake Superior beyond
3   Seating area in the two-story south-facing main lobby

Photography: Ed LaCasse

2

3

4

5

6

St. Mary's Medical Center
Duluth, Minnesota, USA
HKS Architects, Inc.

4 Patients are greeted at a concierge desk on entry as part of the hospital's effort to minimize patient stress
5 Cancer Center reception desk with waiting areas beyond offer calming colors to help allay patient fears
6 Waiting areas and lobbies are organized around the main lobby, which allows daylight and views to permeate deep into the building
Photography: Ed LaCasse

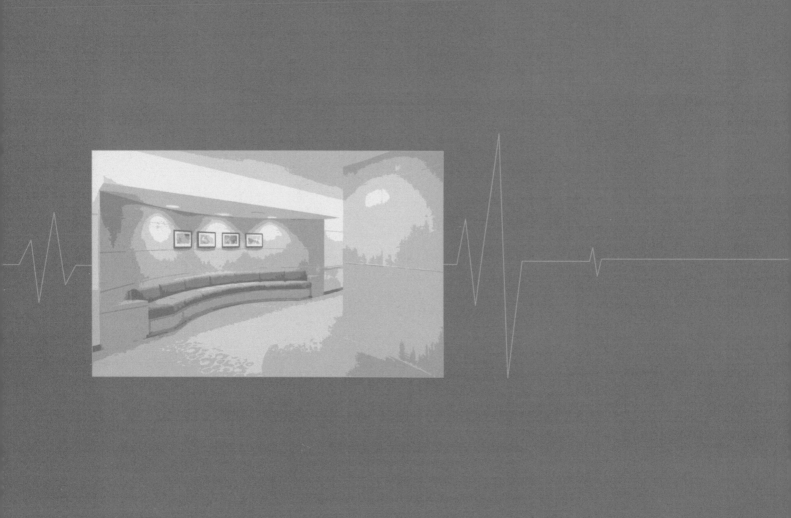

WAITING AREAS

1

2

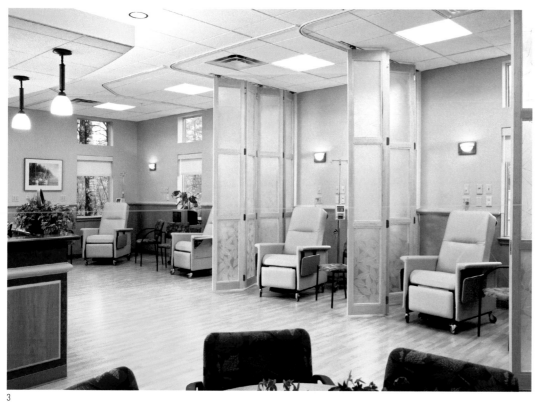

3

Christus Muguerza del Sur
Monterrey, Mexico
HKS Architects, Inc.
1   Soft lighting, wood insets in the flooring, and
     contemporary furniture create a restful atmosphere
Photography: Blake Marvin

Exeter Hospital
Exeter, New Hampshire, USA
JSA Inc.
2   Radiation therapy waiting room
Photography: Blind Dog Photography

Cancer Care Center of York County
Sanford, Maine, USA
JSA Inc.
3   Infusion treatment area aims to provide a calm and
     restful atmosphere. Daylight enters from windows
     at two levels.
Photography: Blind Dog Photography

Laser Clinique Medical Dental Spa
San Diego, California, USA
Saunders + Wiant Architects
4   Subdued interiors with calming views to the
     outdoors help alleviate apprehension
Photography: Ian Wiant

4

Sentara Heart Hospital
Norfolk, Virginia, USA
HDR Architecture, Inc.

1   The use of natural woods and warm-toned colors conveys a sense of peace and tranquillity

Photography: Mark Ballogg

Providence Newberg Medical Center
Newberg, Oregon, USA
Mahlum Architects

2   In using exterior building materials such as brick in adjacent interiors, the beauty of the outdoors is brought in to the public waiting areas. A rich color palette and materials typical of a hospital setting enhance the spaces.

Photography: Benjamin Benschneider

1

Melinda French Gates Ambulatory Care Building
Seattle, Washington, USA
HKS Architects, Inc.

1   Oceanic icons in the terrazzo flooring guide patients and families through various areas
2   The atrium provides multiple seating areas for high-intensity ambulatory care services, the pharmacy, and imaging services behind curved art glass walls for privacy
3   Clinic family reception continues the Puget Sound underwater theme, incorporating positive distractions, performance stages, and custom art glass lighting emulating sea creatures

Photography: Ed LaCasse

2

3

Abbott Northwestern Heart Hospital
Minneapolis, Minnesota, USA
HKS Architects, Inc.

1 Main reception family care center
2 Solarium on fourth floor
3 A family waiting room with adjacent balconies and views of the park
4 Family seating arrangements offer privacy in main waiting area at diagnostic clinics
Photography: Ed LaCasse

1

2

3

4

Ladera Ranch Pediatric Dentistry
Ladera Ranch, California, USA
Saunders + Wiant Architects
1   Woven vinyl "carpet" provides a soft,
    cleanable surface and complements the
    jungle theme
Photography: Ian Wiant

Coastal Kids Children's Medical Group
Newport Beach, California, USA
Saunders + Wiant Architects
2   Beach and boardwalk themes throughout
    add interest
Opposite:
    Contrasting wavy, "underwater" seating
    and play area
Photography: Ian Wiant

1

2

**Clarian West Medical Center
Avon, Indiana, USA**
HKS Architects, Inc.

1 Public concourse provides intuitive
    wayfinding accented by small, private
    waiting areas

Photography: Ed LaCasse

1

Edinburg Children's Hospital
Edinburg, Texas, USA
HKS Architects, Inc.
1   A unique 3-D mural called "Beyond the City" is staged in the main lobby to intrigue and provide positive distractions
2   The menagerie of jungle characters establishes a sense of place for the children's hospital
3   The registration desks offer private seating areas, while the mural's animals further the jungle theme
Photography: Ed LaCasse

1

2

3

Riverview Psychiatric Treatment Center
Augusta, Maine, USA
JSA Inc.

1   Inpatient day room. Abundant natural
    light and panoramic views lessen anxiety.

Photography: Peter Urbanski

Clarian North Medical Center
Carmel, Indiana, USA
HKS Architects, Inc.

2   Patient/family retreat provides a
    soothing, homelike environment

Photography: Jeff Millies, Hedrich Blessing
Photography

Bloorview Kids Rehab
Toronto, Ontario, Canada
Montgomery Sisam Architects / Stantec
Architecture

3   Paneled roof, overhead lighting and
    suspended sculpture provides a perfect
    backdrop for patients and families to
    access computers

Photography: Tom Arban Photography

2

1

2

3

Parker Adventist Hospital
Parker, Colorado, USA
HKS Architects, Inc.
1   The waiting areas offer families a place of respite while waiting for news on loved ones
2   Dining room views are oriented toward Pike's Peak
3   Waiting areas are designed to be warm and inviting
Photography: Ed LaCasse

Town & Country Medical Spa
Houston, Texas, USA
Kirksey Architects

1   Reception area and waiting room. Large sofas, plumped pillows, wall print and plants make it a true "home away from home."
2&3   Soft overhead lighting, recessed alcoves and elegant furniture provide luxury and comfort
Photography: Hester & Hardaway Photography

1

2

3

1

St. Mary's Medical Center
Duluth, Minnesota, USA
HKS Architects, Inc.
1   A calming palette of soft gray for carpets and furnishing and buff for
    the walls helps create a comfortable waiting area
2   Large glass panes allow views to the outdoors
3   Waiting areas overlook the scenic landscape including Lake Superior
Photography: Ed LaCasse

3

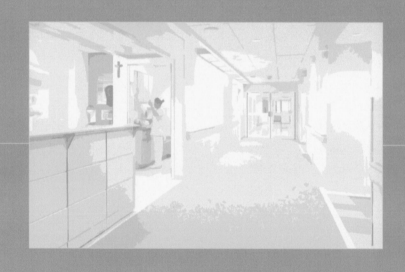

NURSES' STATIONS AND CORRIDORS

1

2

Exeter Hospital
Exeter, New Hampshire, USA
JSA Inc.
1   Emergency department
2   Birthing center
Photography: Blind Dog Photography

McKay-Dee Hospital Center
Ogden, Utah, USA
HKS Architects, Inc.
3   Nurse work areas off corridor allow direct
    visibility to the Intensive Care Unit rooms
4   Carpeted corridors in nurse work areas
    reduce noise and institutional feel
Photography: Blake Marvin

3

4

2

**Melinda French Gates Ambulatory Care Building
Seattle, Washington, USA**
HKS Architects, Inc.
Opposite:
　Clinic patients are greeted at each entrance from the family reception
　by a caregiver workstation reinforcing interior wayfinding
2　Painted portholes resembling views out into the ocean are dotted
　along each corridor
3　Original photography reinforced by floor medallions punctuate
　corridor intersections accented by cove lighting
Photography: Ed LaCasse

3

Abbott Northwestern Heart Hospital
Minneapolis, Minnesota, USA
HKS Architects, Inc.

1   Natural wood in the patient care corridors provides warmth to clinical spaces
2   Nurses' station and adjacent waiting room on the fifth floor
3   Bedside supplies and documentation offer safety aspects to design

Photography: Ed LaCasse

1

2

3

The Wisconsin Heart Hospital
Wauwatosa, Wisconsin, USA
HDR Architecture, Inc.

1&2 The hospital utilizes a "universal bed" approach, where patients use one private room during their entire stay and resources are brought to the patient rather than moving the patient between different departments

Photography: Mark Ballogg

1

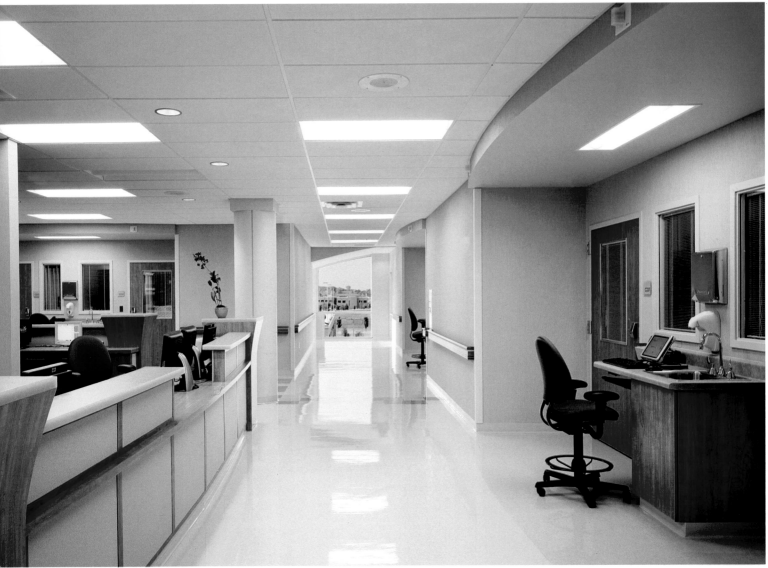

2

3

West Coast Radiology Center
Laguna Niguel, California, USA
Saunders + Wiant Architects

3 A sinewy hallway leads patients
   back to the imaging areas

Photography: Ian Wiant

Millennium Dental
Sherman Oaks, California, USA
Abramson Teiger Architects

4 Curved lines and soft color provides
   a calming feel to the hall leading to
   consulting rooms

Photography: Douglas Olson Photography

Laser Clinique Medical Spa
San Diego, California, USA
Saunders + Wiant Architects

5 Flowing, softly lit routes lead
   patients through the facility

Photography: Niall Saunders

4   5

1

2

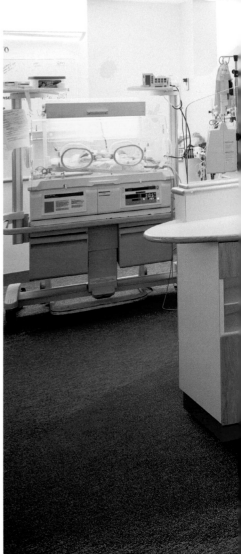

3

Children's Hospital
Omaha, Nebraska, USA
HDR Architecture, Inc.

1–3 Nurses have workstations with views to the patient
       rooms. Locked supply carts and servidoors ensure
       easy access to supplies.

Photography: Tom Kessler Photography

2

Clarian West Medical Center
Avon, Indiana, USA
HKS Architects, Inc.

1   Decentralized nursing stations provide views to patients, computer patient charting and access to supplies below
2   Playful colors and a curvilinear design add visual appeal to the pediatric concourse

Photography: Ed LaCasse

2

Lantern Bend Medical Office Building
Houston, Texas, USA
Kirksey Architecture

1   Hallway

Photography: Aker/Zvonkovic Photography

Sentara Heart Hospital
Norfolk, Virginia, USA
HDR Architecture, Inc

2&3   Dynamic and functional nursing stations allow
       for enhanced visibility into patient rooms and
       treatment areas

Photography: Mark Ballogg

3

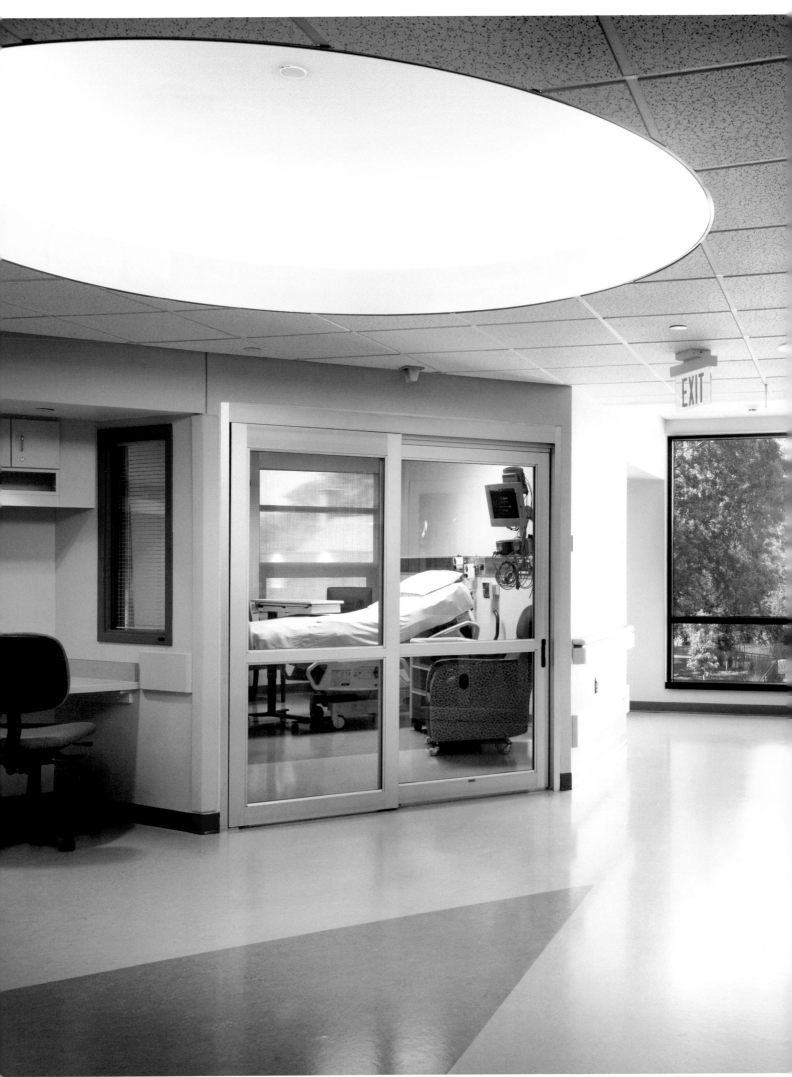

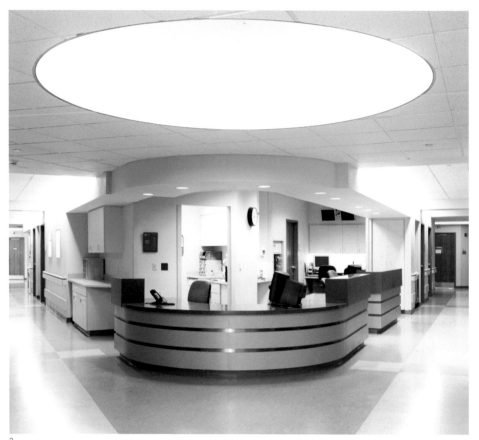

Washington Regional Medical Center
Fayetteville, Arkansas, USA
HKS Architects, Inc.

1   The Critical Care Unit includes wide, easy-to-navigate hallways and large windows to allow natural lighting
2   Central core stations support the nursing floors
Photography: Ed LaCasse

2

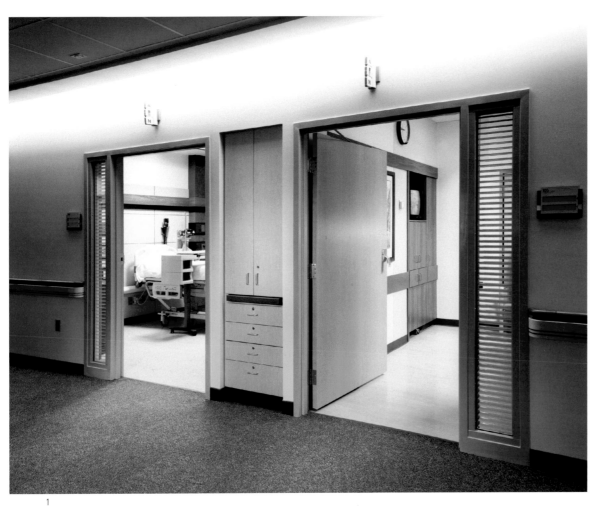

1

3

2

4

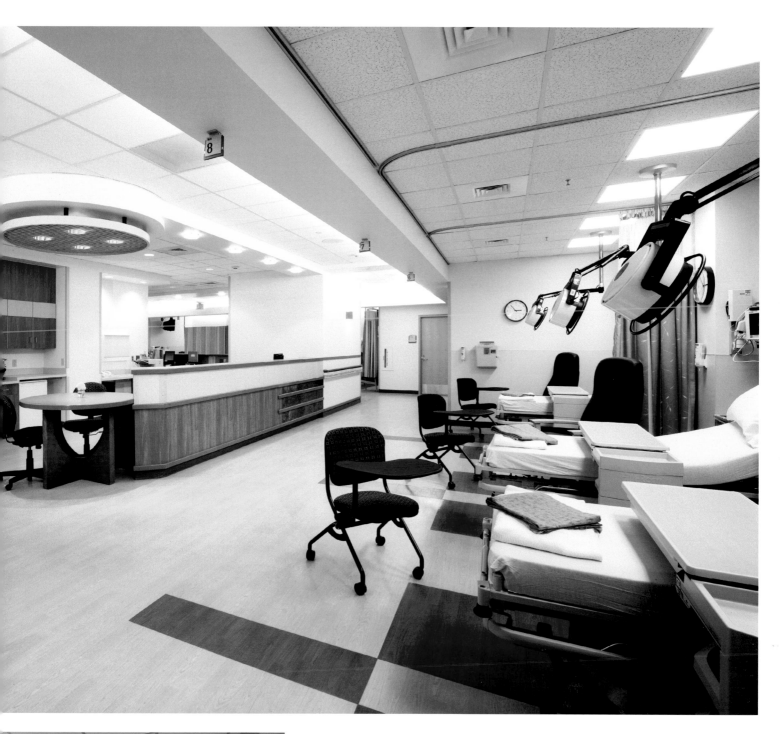

Parker Adventist Hospital
Parker, Colorado, USA
HKS Architects, Inc.

1   Private patient rooms are supported with substations located between rooms
2   Practical layout of counters enable easy monitoring of rooms
3   Wooden floors and accents impart a warm feel to the area
4   Floor detail and lighting accent adds interest to this area
Photography: Ed LaCasse

Parker Adventist Hospital
Parker, Colorado, USA
HKS Architects, Inc.

5 Creating a cadence through floor patterning helps shorten the feel of long corridors

6 View of sterile corridor with scrub sinks located next to each operating room

7 Providing visual stimulation for the pediatric population allows positive distractions

Photography: Ed LaCasse

5

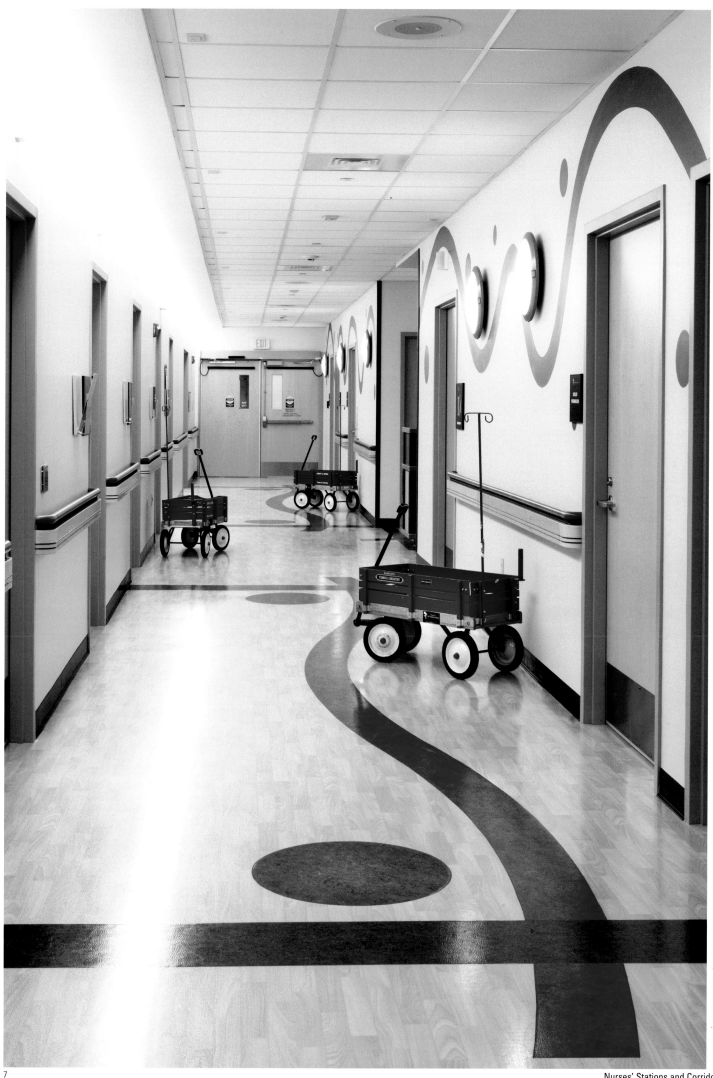

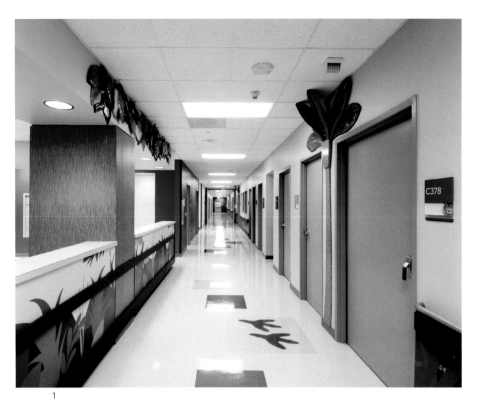

1

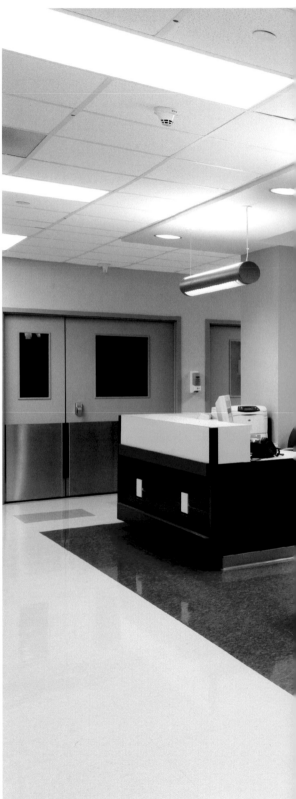

3

Edinburg Children's Hospital
Edinburg, Texas, USA
HKS Architects, Inc.
1   Bright colors and a jungle theme provide distractions for children during their visit
2   Three-dimensional palm tree room dividers and animal-track wayfinding devices
    lend playfulness to the interior of the children's hospital
3   Spacious reception/nurses' station area facilitates monitoring of patients
Photography: Ed LaCasse

Christus Muguerza del Sur
Monterrey, Mexico
HKS Architects, Inc.
1   Special colored nodes draw attention to room entrances along corridors
2   Vinyl flooring in the emergency department helps provide a clean and sterile area
3   Room entrances are recessed to give a sense of identity
4   Hallways are carpeted to help with sound attenuation
Photography: Blake Marvin

1

2

3

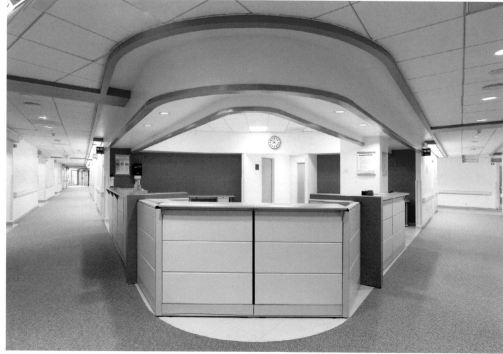

4

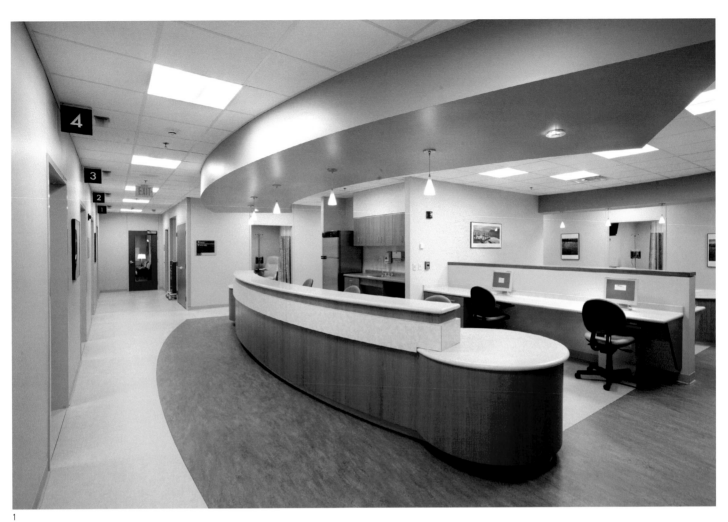

1

St. Mary's Medical Center
Duluth, Minnesota, USA
HKS Architects, Inc.
1&2 Open nurse's station promotes family interaction with
       nurses and other staff
Photography: Ed LaCasse

Baptist Health Medical Center
North Little Rock, Arkansas, USA
HKS Architects, Inc.
3&4 Nurses' station conveniently located at a corridor corner
       to promote optimum visibility
Photography: King Graf

3

4

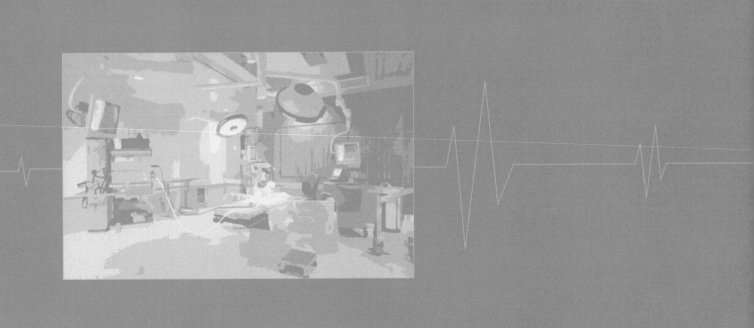

DIAGNOSTIC, SURGICAL, AND RECOVERY AREAS

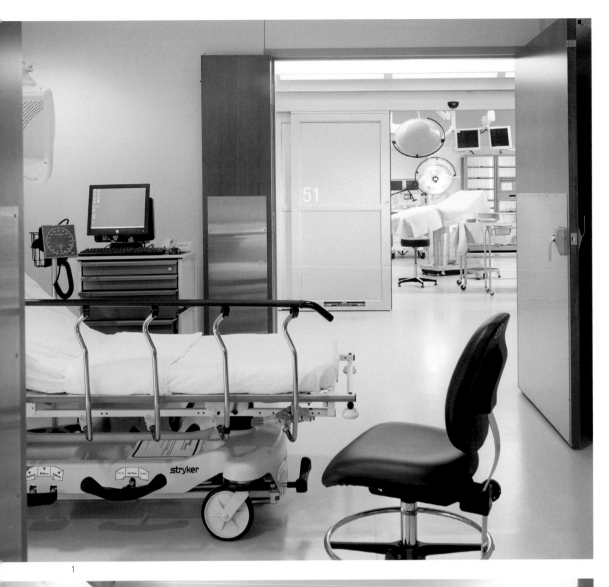

1

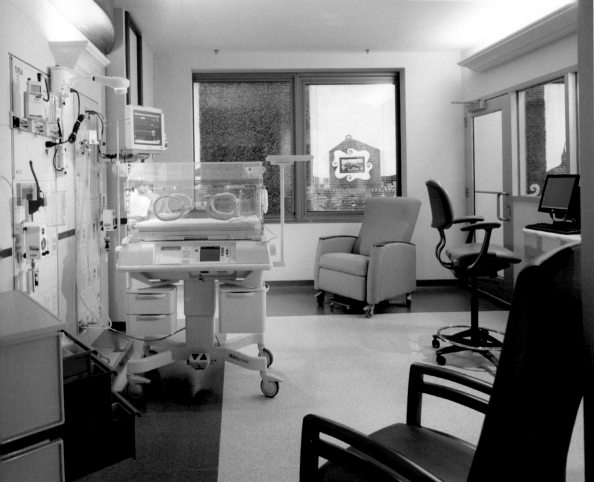

2

3

Beaumont Surgical Learning Center
Royal Oak, Michigan, USA
Harley Ellis Devereaux
  1   Pre and post-operative rooms are located directly across from surgical suites
2&3 Private NICU rooms have specialized acoustic panels along with adjustable light and air controls
Photography: Justin Maconochie Photography

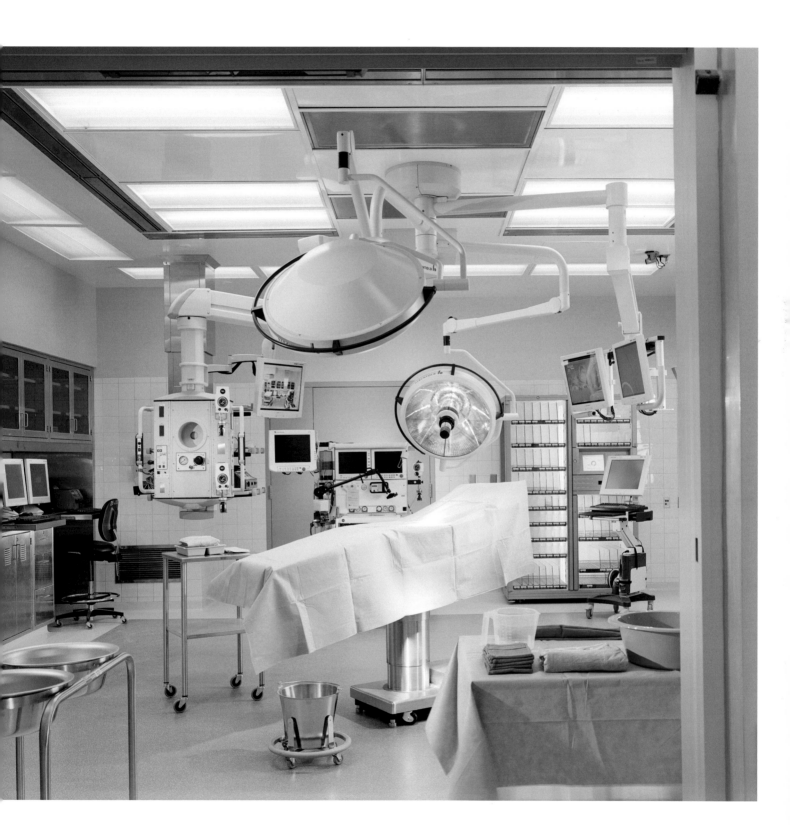

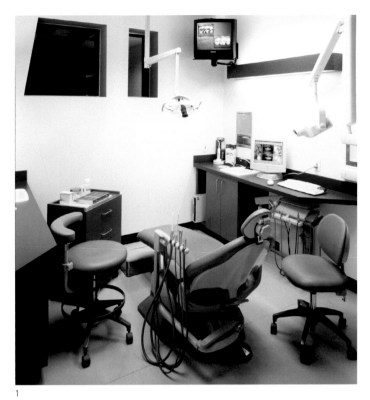

1

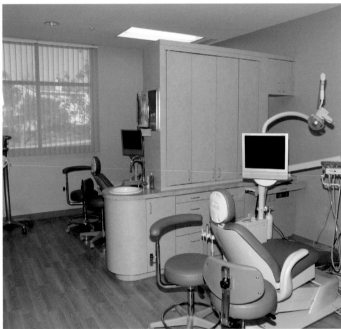

2

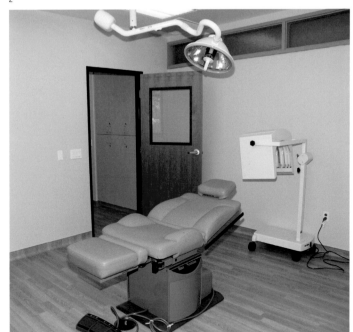

3

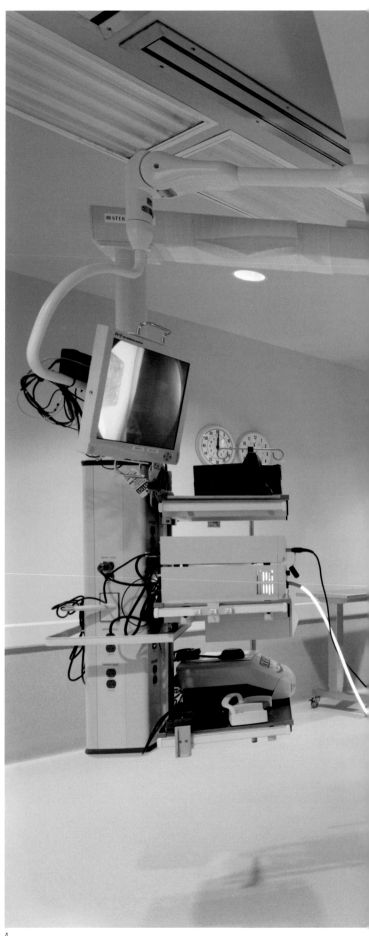

4

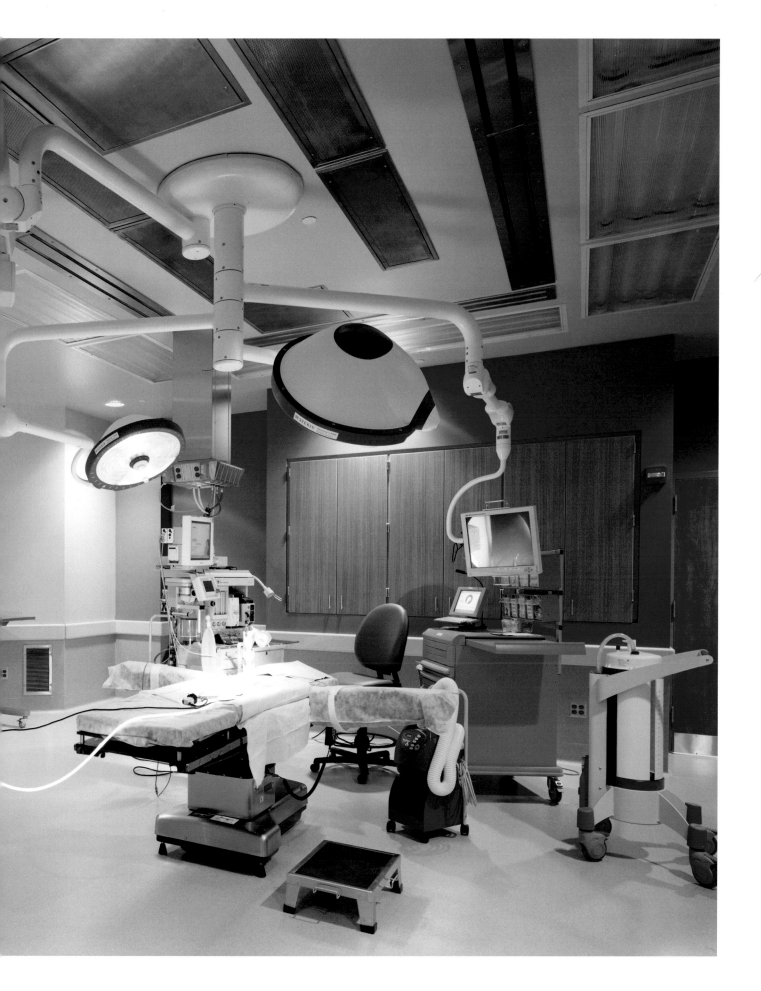

Millennium Dental
Sherman Oaks, California, USA
Abramson Teiger Architects

1   Ergonomically designed consulting room
    is accented with calm blue colors

Photography: Douglas Olson Photography

Laser Clinique Medical Spa
San Diego, California, USA
Saunders + Wiant Architecture

2   Dental stations

3   Cosmetic spa procedure room

Photography: Niall Saunders

Providence Newberg Medical Center
Newberg, Oregon, USA
Mahlum Architects

4   This entire LEED Gold-rated facility including the
    most intense inpatient areas of surgery employs
    a mechanical system that uses 100 percent outside
    air for infection control and efficient operation

Photography: Eckert & Eckert

1

2

**Abbott Northwestern Heart Hospital
Minneapolis, Minnesota, USA**
HKS Architects, Inc.

1   Full-height walls and glass breakaway
    doors maximize privacy in the cath lab
    and surgical pre/post-operations area

2   Integrated MRA provides real-time
    diagnoses within the heart hospital

3   Natural light, artworks, and family
    seating at cath lab prep/recovery
    address the patients' needs
    throughout their experience

4   Four-bed pod at CVICU was designed
    for optimum patient visibility

5   CVICU pods maximize visibility and
    safety for patients

Photography: Ed LaCasse

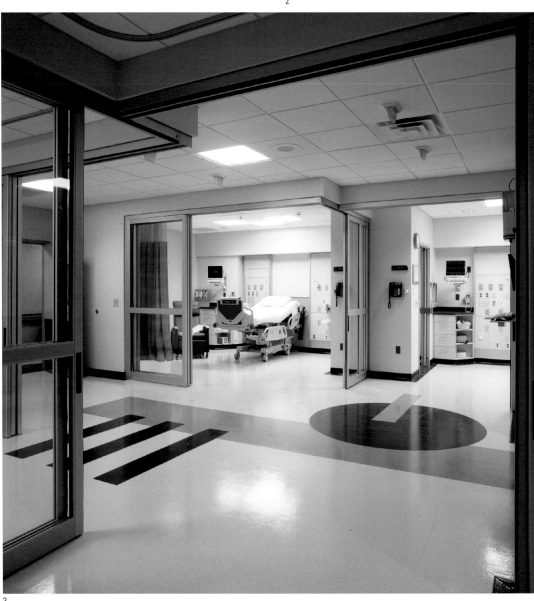

3

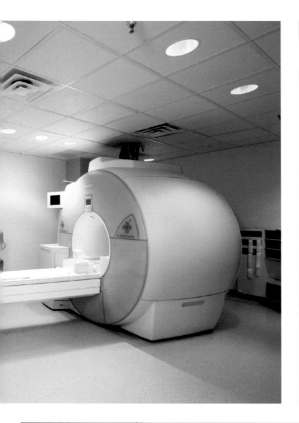

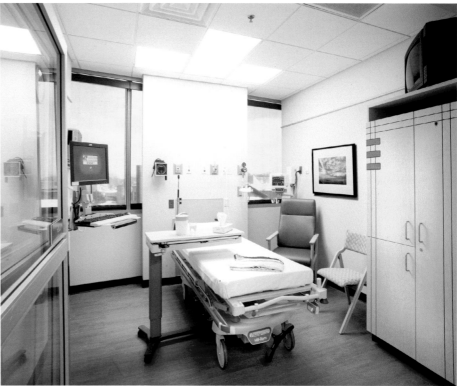

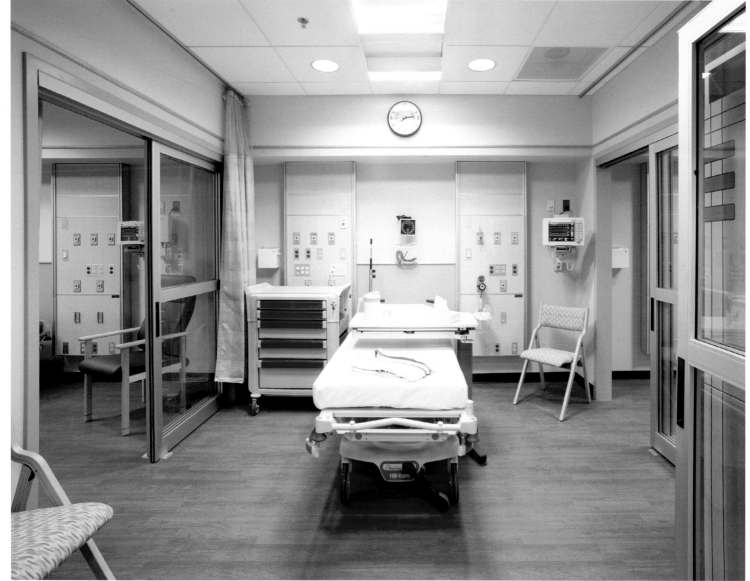

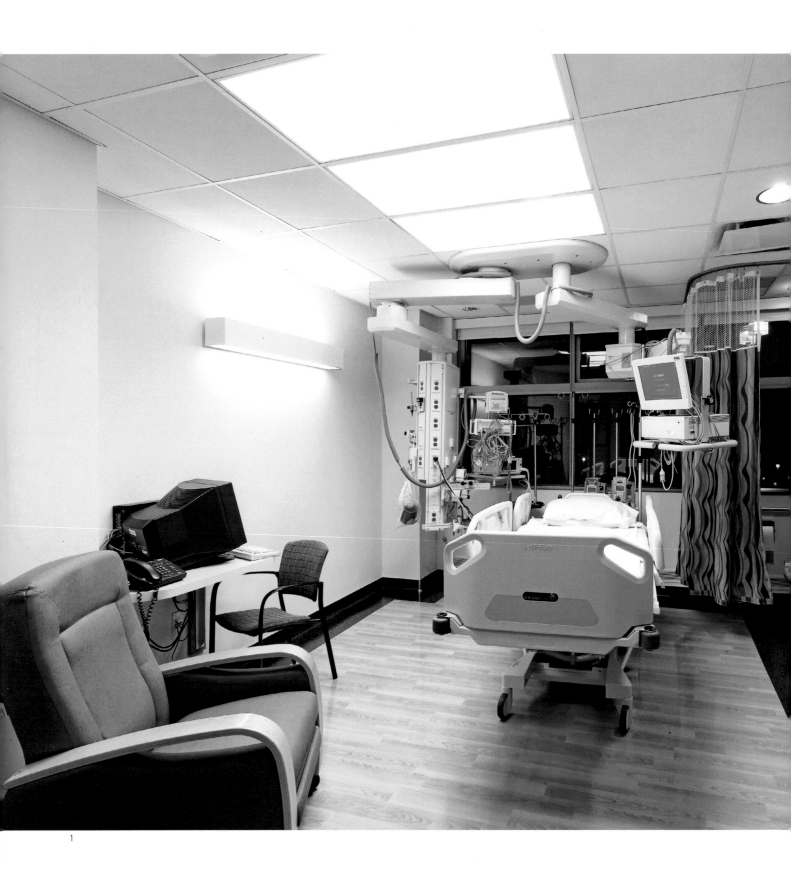

1

McKay-Dee Hospital Center
Ogden, Utah, USA
HKS Architects, Inc.

1   Expansive daylighting, mountain views, and
    the warm texture of the floor counteract the
    high-tech feel of the intensive care unit

Photography: Blake Marvin

Renown Health South Meadows
Diagnostic and Treatment Pavilion
Reno, Nevada, USA
HMC Architects

2   Surgery recovery beds
3   Operating room
4   CT Scanner Control Room; looking
    into the machine

Photography: Vance Fox

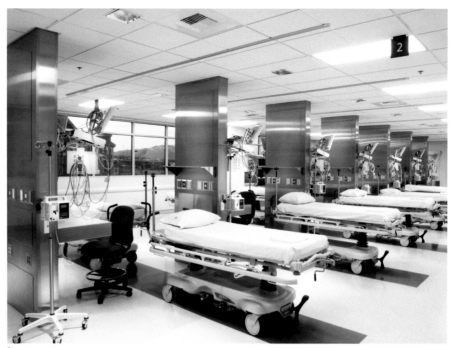

2

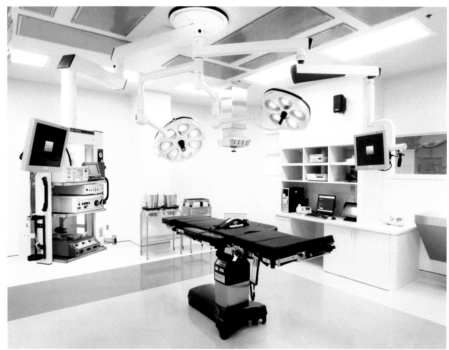

3

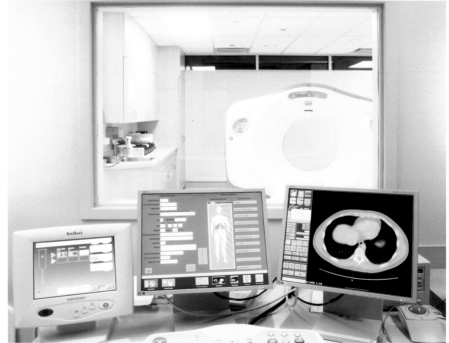

4

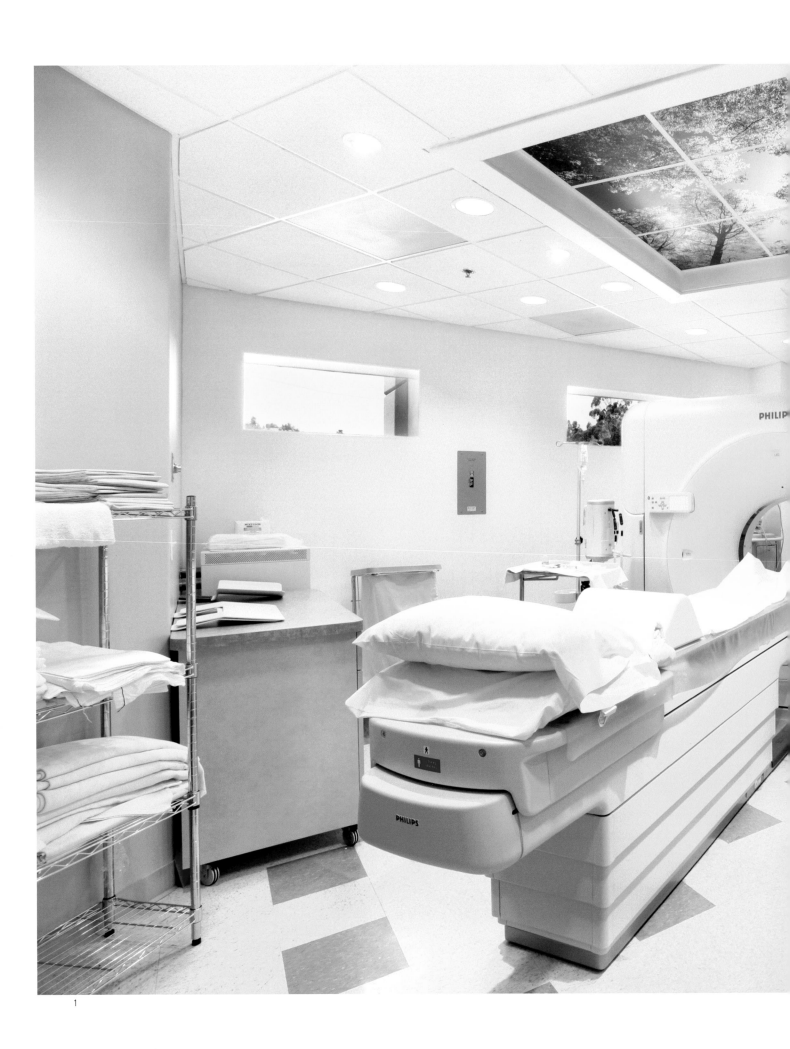

1

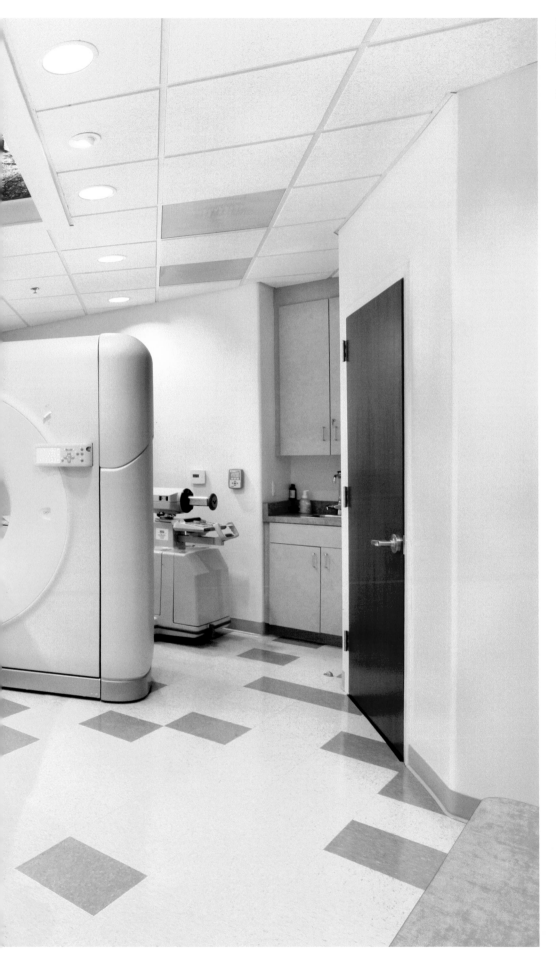

West Coast Radiology Center
Laguna Niguel, California, USA
Saunders + Wiant Architects

1   Computed tomography (CT) imaging suite
     combines light and vistas to enhance
     patient comfort

Photography: Ian Wiant

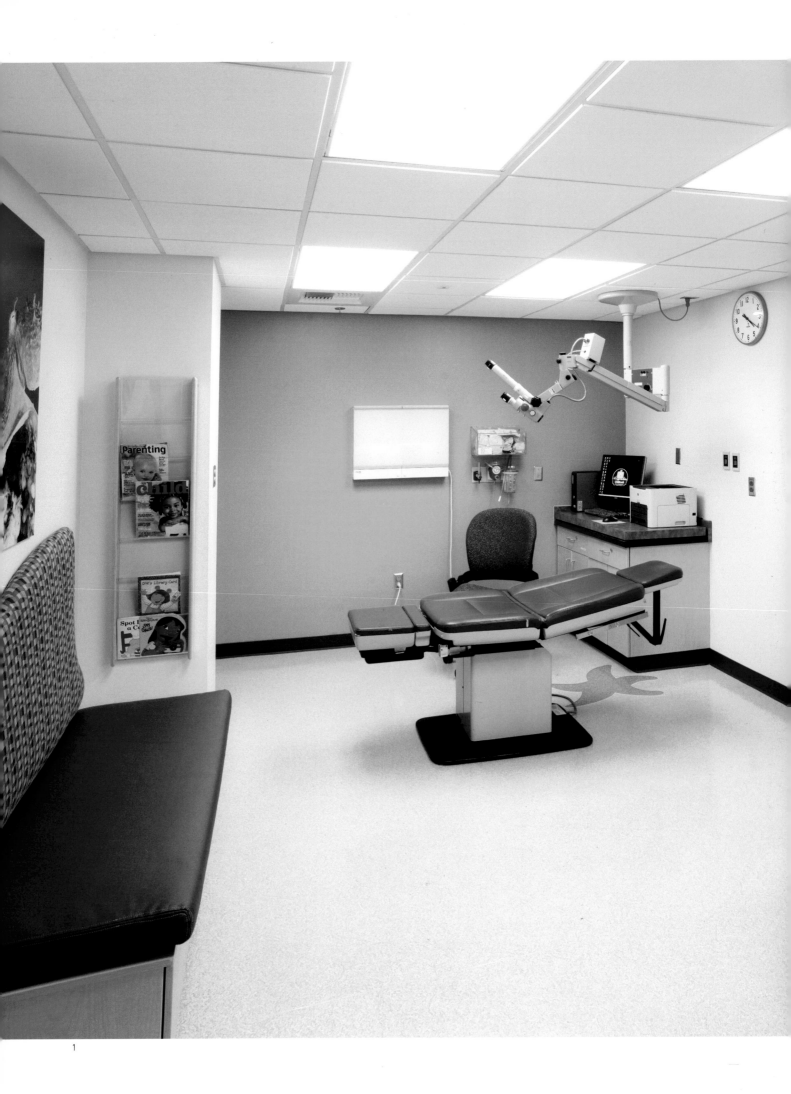

1

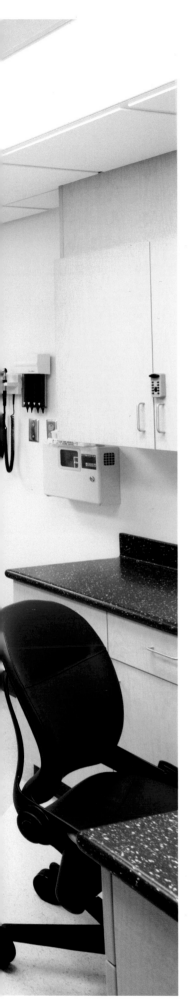

**Melinda French Gates Ambulatory Care Building
Seattle, Washington, USA**
HKS Architects, Inc.

1   Ocean theme on floor carries through to offer a playful
    element in the examination room
2   Custom art glass sconces depicting ocean themes become
    the art for the examination and treatment rooms
Photography: Ed LaCasse

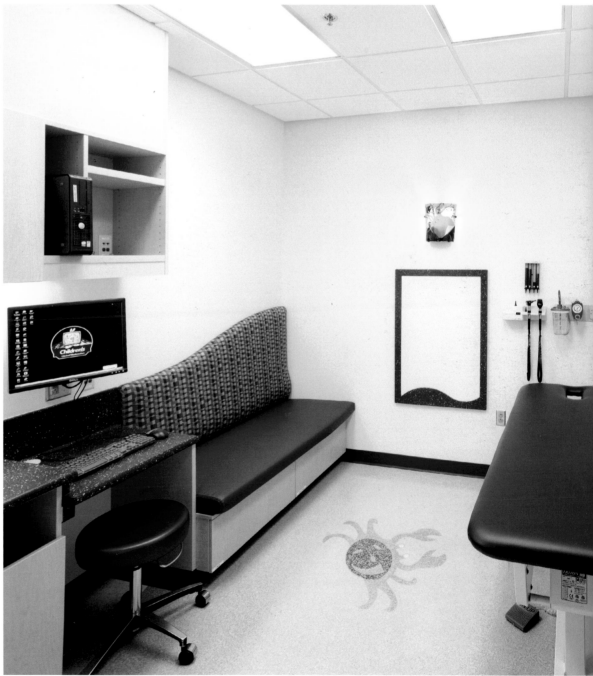

2

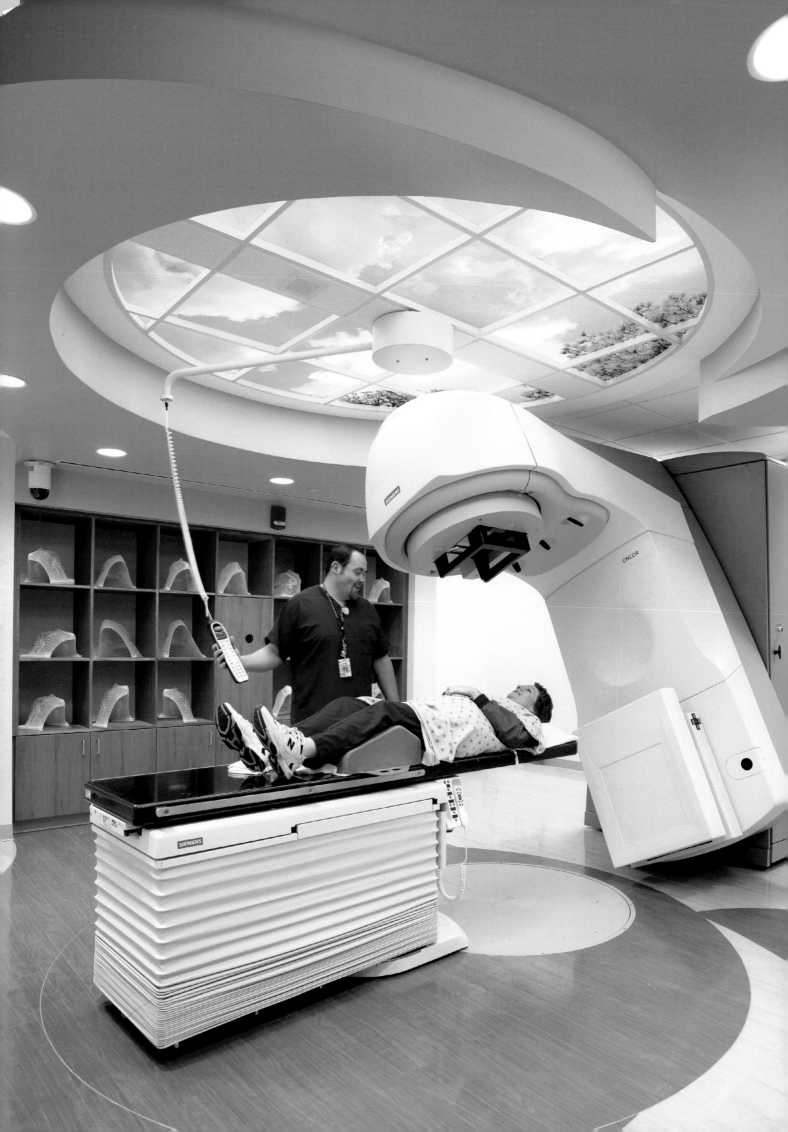

2

Firelands Regional Medical Center
Sandusky, Ohio, USA
Harley Ellis Devereaux

Opposite:
   This comprehensive Cancer Center is a complete
   facility for patients and their families

Photography: Steve Maylone Photography

Exeter Hospital
Exeter, New Hampshire, USA
JSA Inc.

2   Linear Accelerator Vault. Interesting lighting
    responds to the patient's view upward during
    treatment.

Photography: Blind Dog Photography

Coastal Kids Children's Medical Group
Newport Beach, California, USA
Saunders + Wiant Architects
1&2 Soft, clean colors and swirling floor patterns in examination
rooms present a lively feel to these spaces
Photography: Ian Wiant

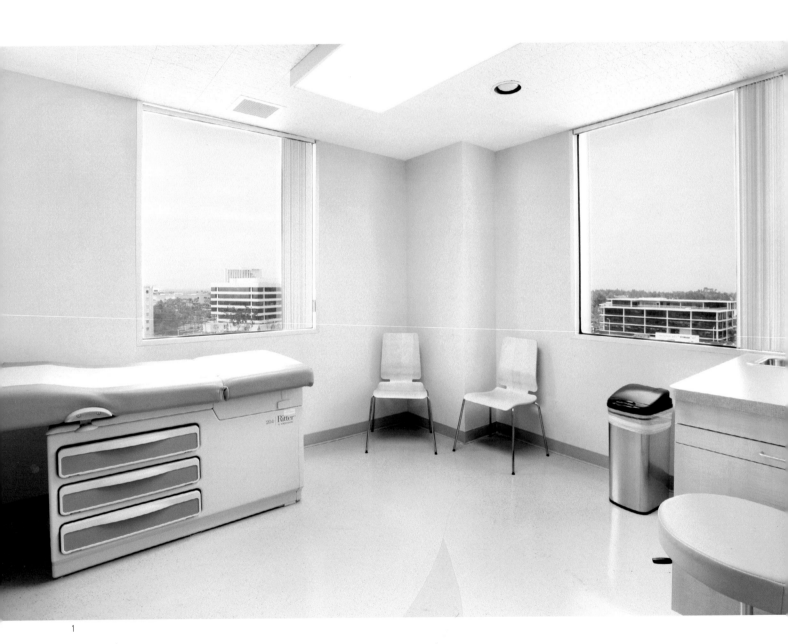

1

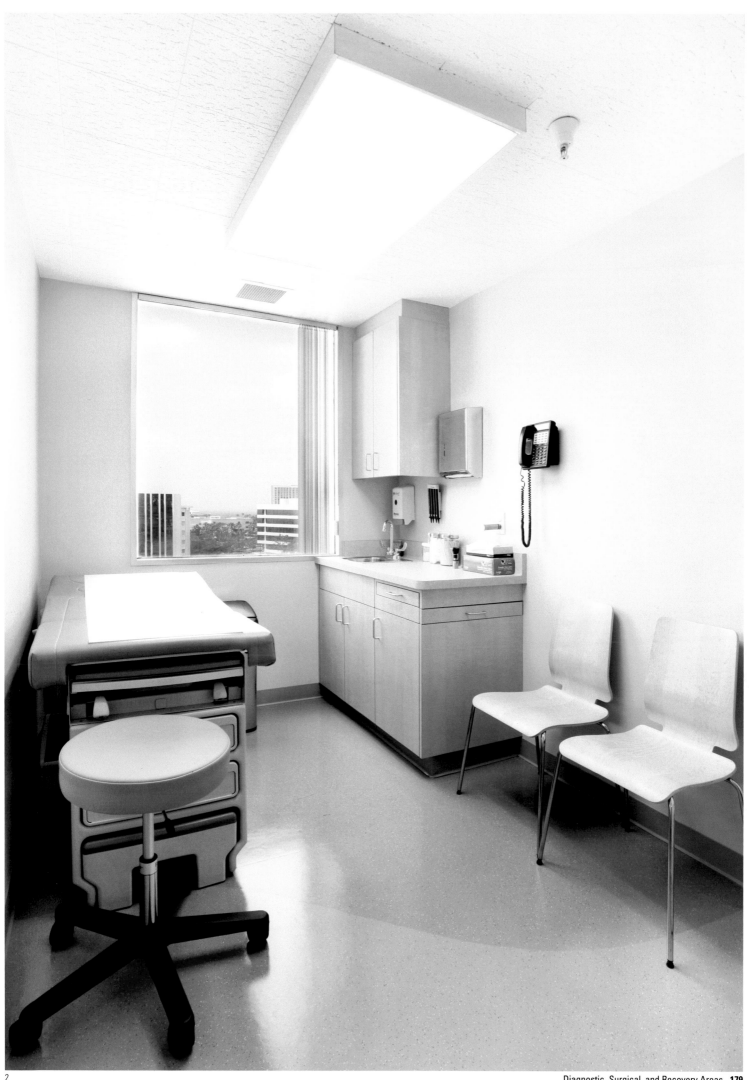

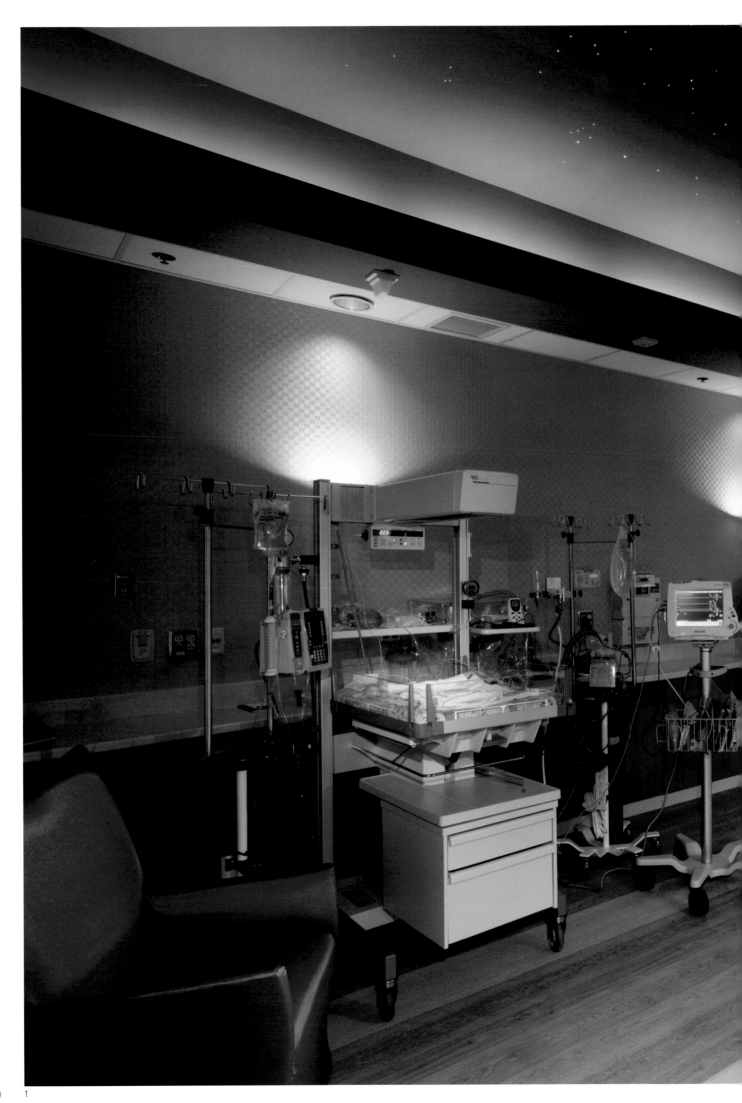

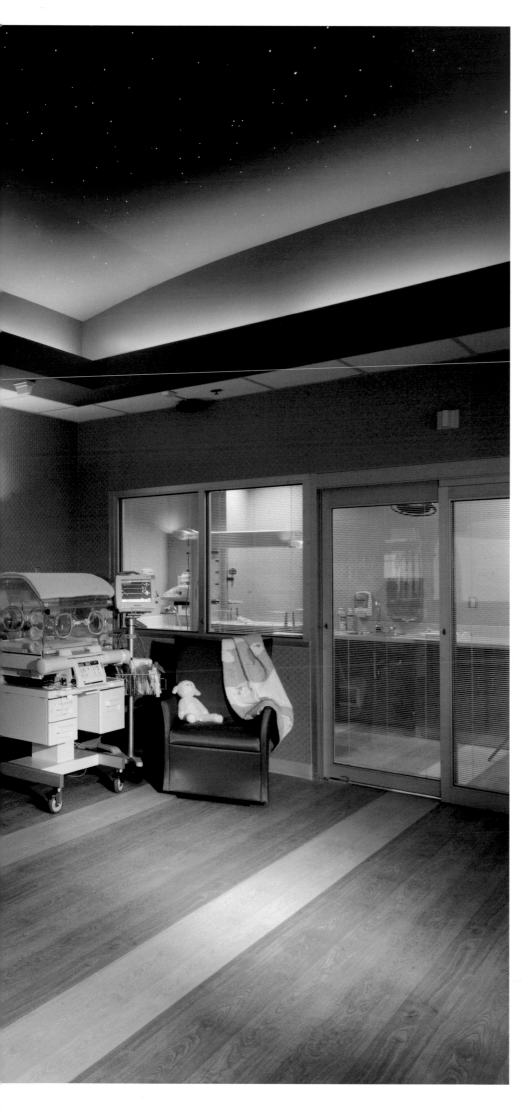

Clarian West Medical Center
Avon, Indiana, USA
HKS Architects, Inc.
1   Speciality lighting enhances the environment for infant, family, and staff in the Special Care Nursery
Photography: Ed LaCasse

1

Clear Image Dental and Medical Spa
Mission Viejo, California, USA
Saunders + Wiant Architects
1   Cool, sleek modernity defines the dental and wellness spa, which
    caters to cosmetic dentistry, facial treatments, and massage therapy
2&3 Contemporary furniture and comfortable massage beds make for
    restful spaces that promote the feeling of well-being
Photography: Ian Wiant

2

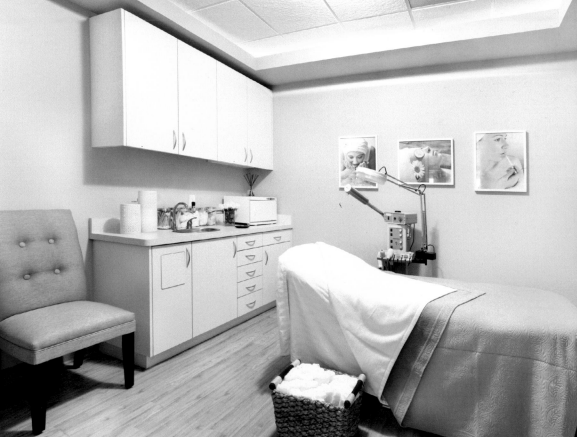

3

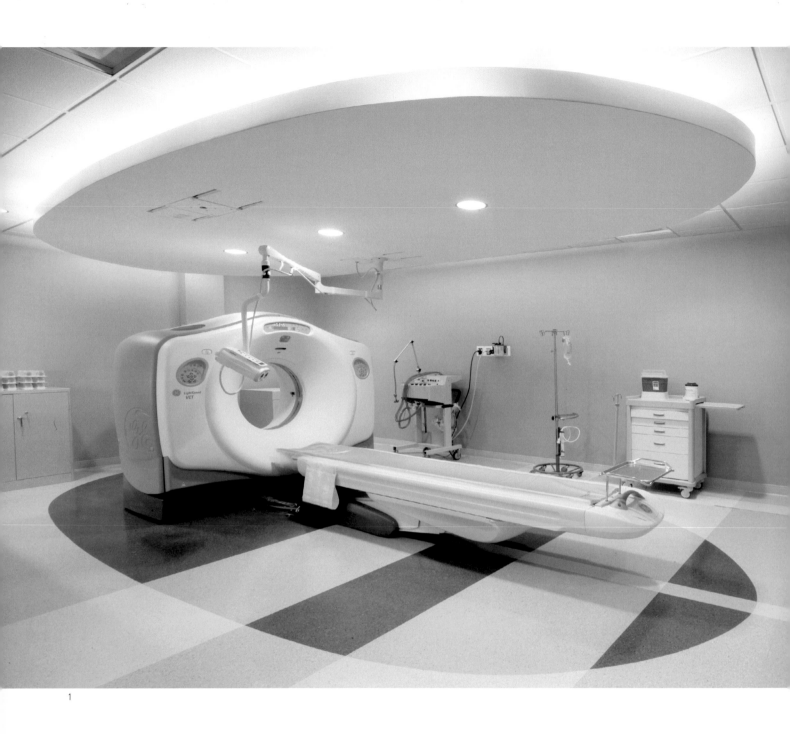

1

Sentara Heart Hospital
Norfolk, Virginia, USA
HDR Architecture, Inc.

1   Sentara offers cutting-edge diagnostic
    capabilities. This 64-slice CT scanner
    provides crisp digital images of coronary
    arteries that previously required invasive
    procedures to view.

Photography: Mark Ballogg

Cancer Care Center of York County
Sanford, Maine, USA
JSA Inc.

2   Linear accelerator vault

Photography: Blind Dog Photography

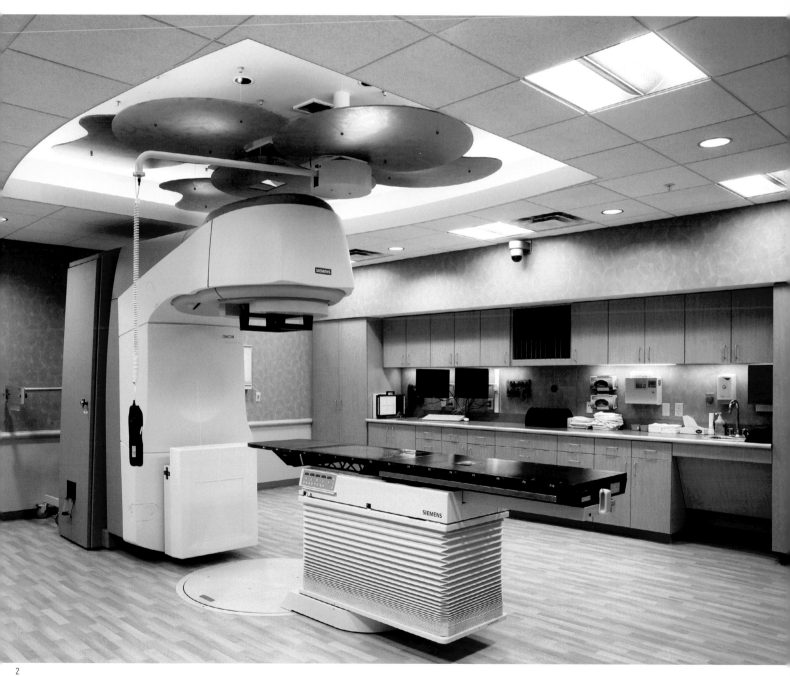

2

Ladera Ranch Pediatric Dentistry
Ladera Ranch, California, USA
Saunders + Wiant Architects

1   Kids entering the dental treatment area
find open-ended features such as the
jungle murals and Banyan tree, which
offer a sense of adventure and mystery

Photography: Ian Wiant

1

Beaumont Surgical Learning Center
Royal Oak, Michigan, USA
Harley Ellis Devereaux
1&2   This state-of-the-art center allows surgeons and students
        to practice everything from suturing to neurosurgery
Photography: Steve Maylone Photography

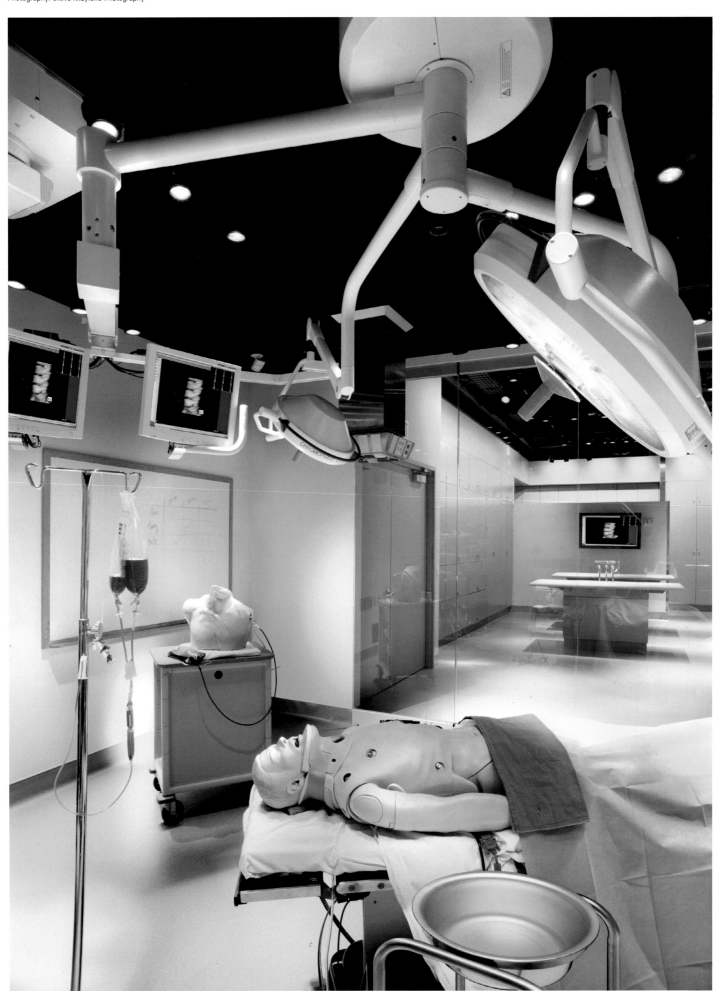

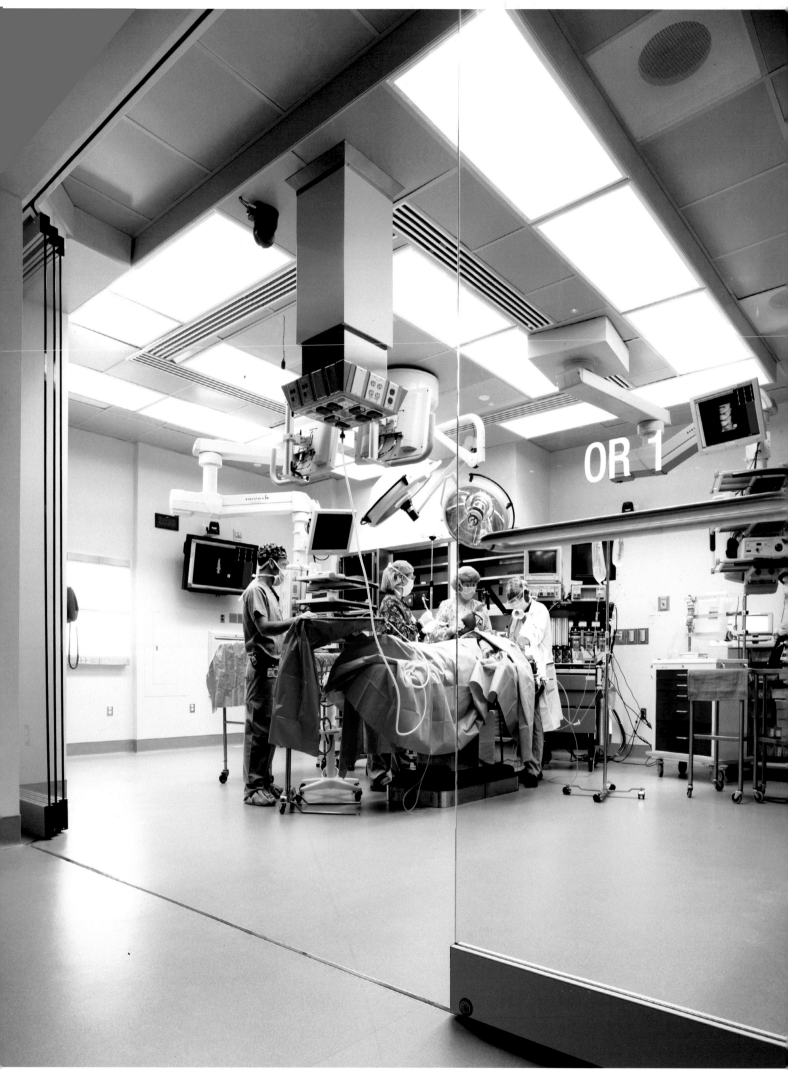

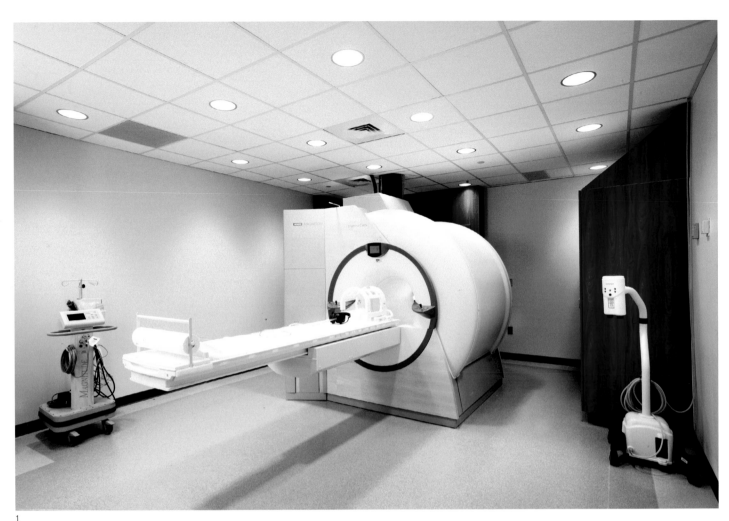

1

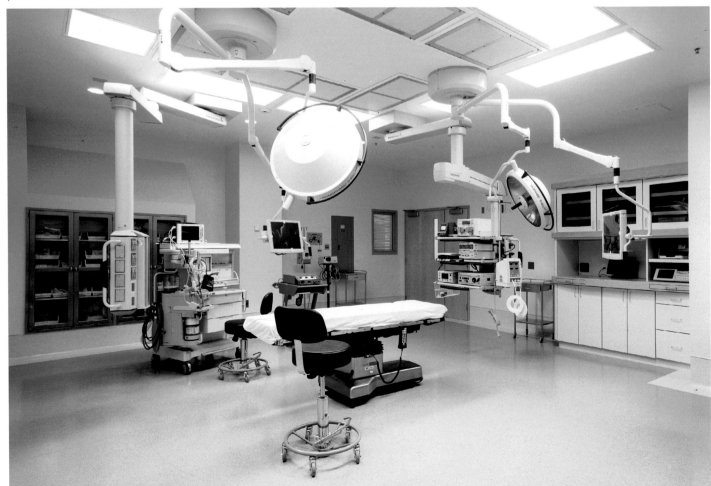

Parker Adventist Hospital
Parker, Colorado, USA
HKS Architects, Inc.
1 Advanced technologies help provide the latest in care while warm wood tones help set patients at ease
2 Ceiling-mounted booms allow doctors to move about freely during surgery
3 High-speed CT is optimally positioned for maximum staff observation of patients to promote safety
Photography: Ed LaCasse

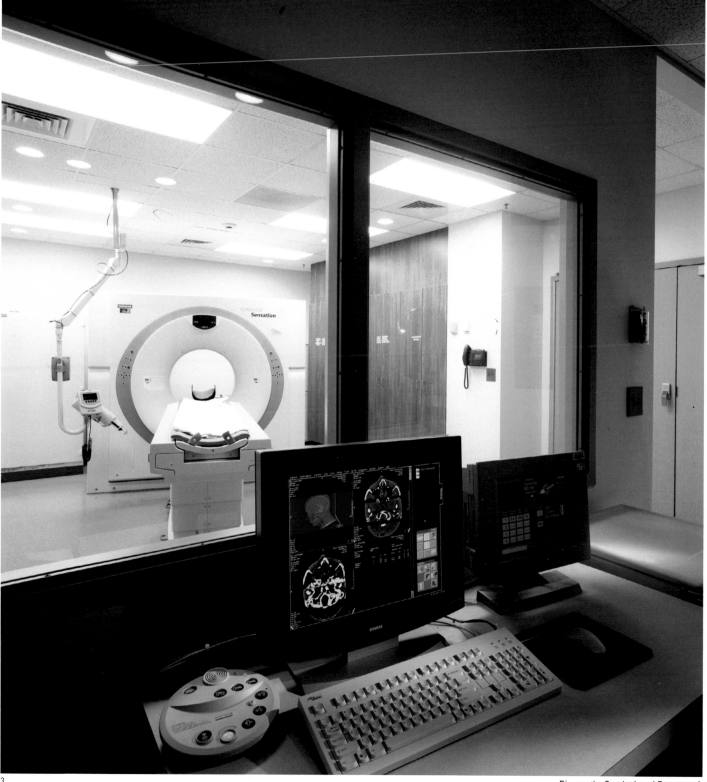

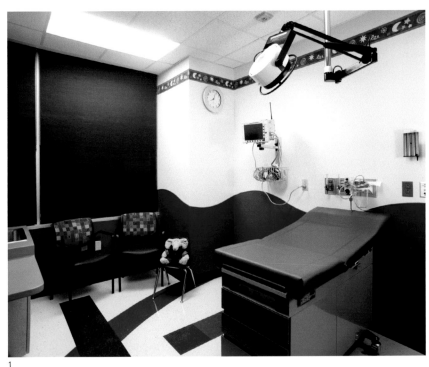

1

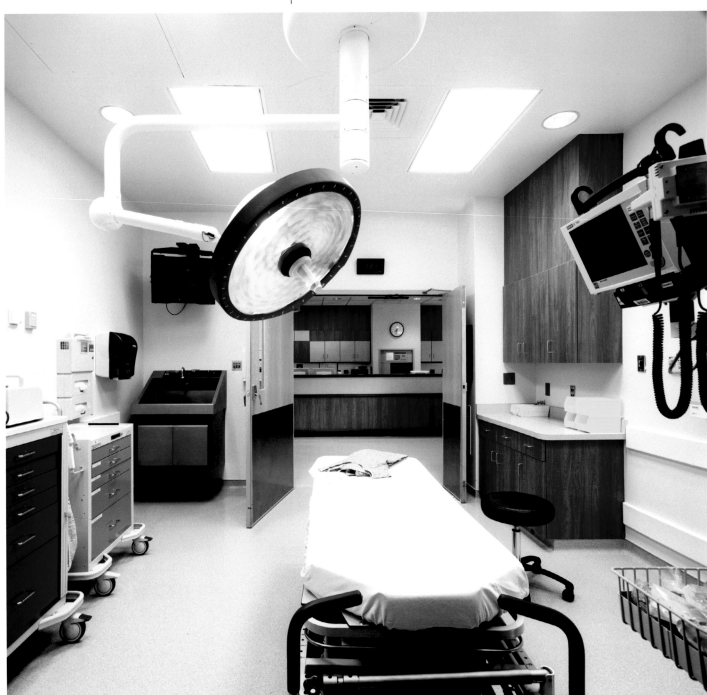

Parker Adventist Hospital
Parker, Colorado, USA
HKS Architects, Inc.

1   Wall and floor patterns with vivid colors
    provide visual interest for pediatric patients
2   Emergency department resuscitation room
    with direct view from the nurse station
Photography: Ed LaCasse

Christus Muguerza del Sur
Monterrey, Mexico
HKS Architects, Inc.

3   Moveable and ceiling-mounted equipment aid
    in a thorough cleaning of the obstetrics rooms
Photography: Blake Marvin

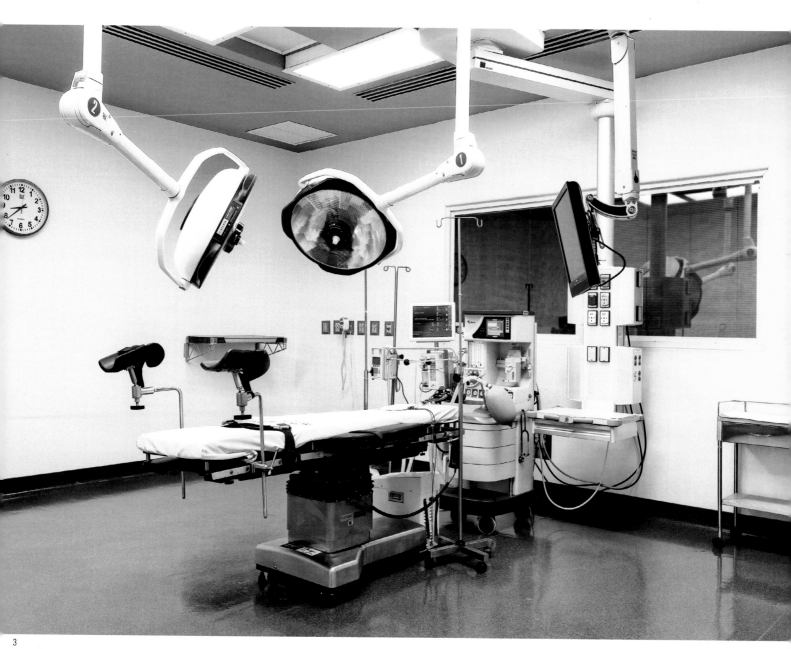

3

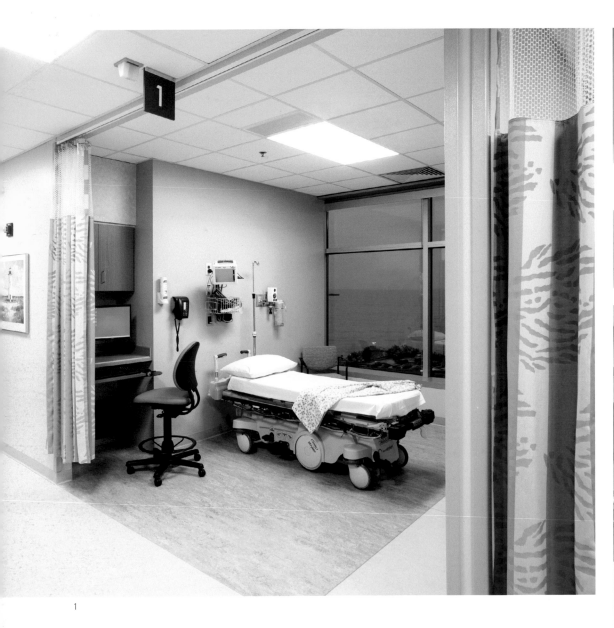

1

2

St. Mary's Medical Center
Duluth, Minnesota, USA
HKS Architects, Inc.
1   Pre-post op recovery station with visual connectivity to Lake Superior
2   Caregiver visibility for multiple patients is achieved through the use of open recovery bays
Photography: Ed LaCasse

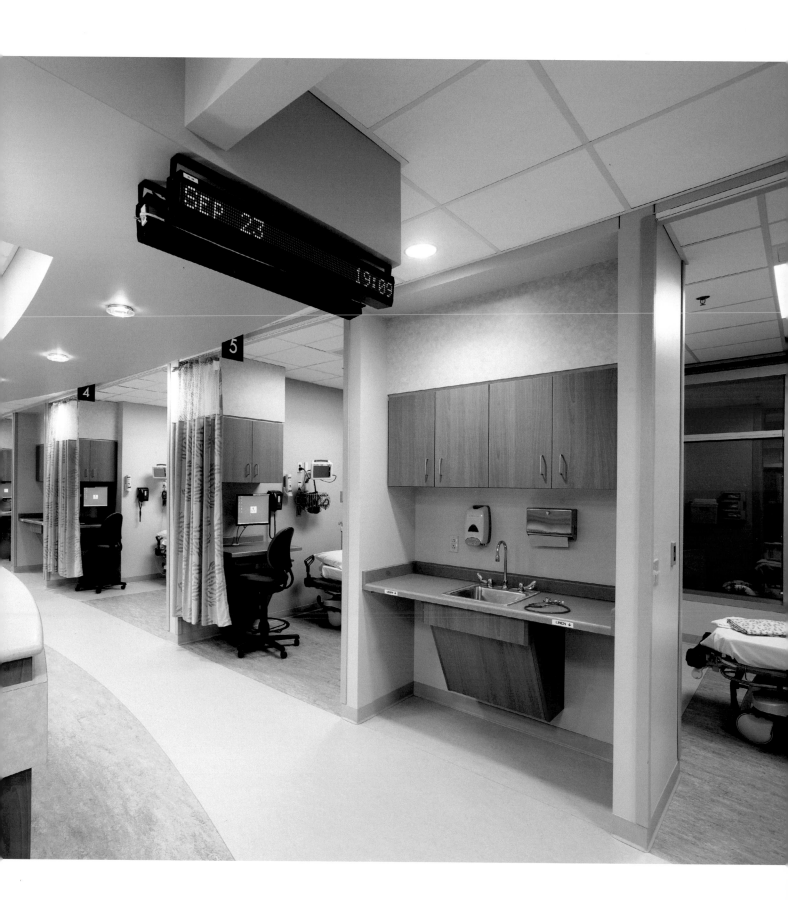

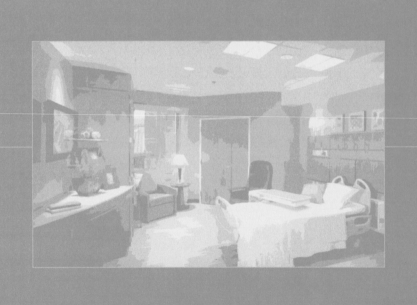

PATIENT ROOMS

**Sentara Heart Hospital
Norfolk, Virginia, USA**
HDR Architecture, Inc.

1   Comfortable patient rooms have computer hook-ups and wireless Internet access. Fold-out sofas allow family members to spend the night.

Photography: Mark Ballogg

**The Wisconsin Heart Hospital
Wauwatosa, Wisconsin, USA**
HDR Architecture, Inc.

2   Medical gases, fold-away patient monitors, supplies, and patient storage are located in custom headwalls and footwalls. Room amenities include wide windows, custom draperies, and sconce lighting. Each room is also equipped with high-speed Internet access and flat-screen technology.

Photography: Mark Ballogg

**Exeter Hospital
Exeter, New Hampshire, USA**
JSA Inc.

Opposite:
    Patient rooms are pleasantly furnished and have inspiring views to the outdoors

Photography: Blind Dog Photography

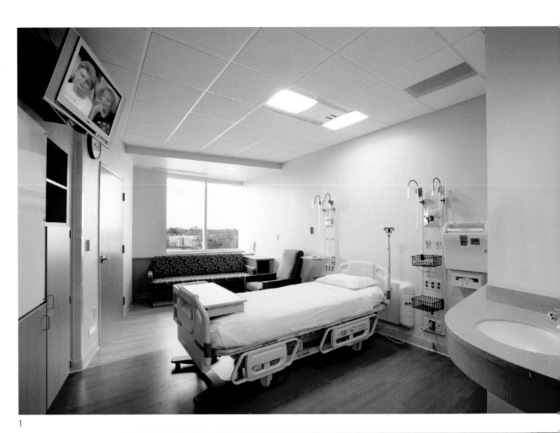

1

2

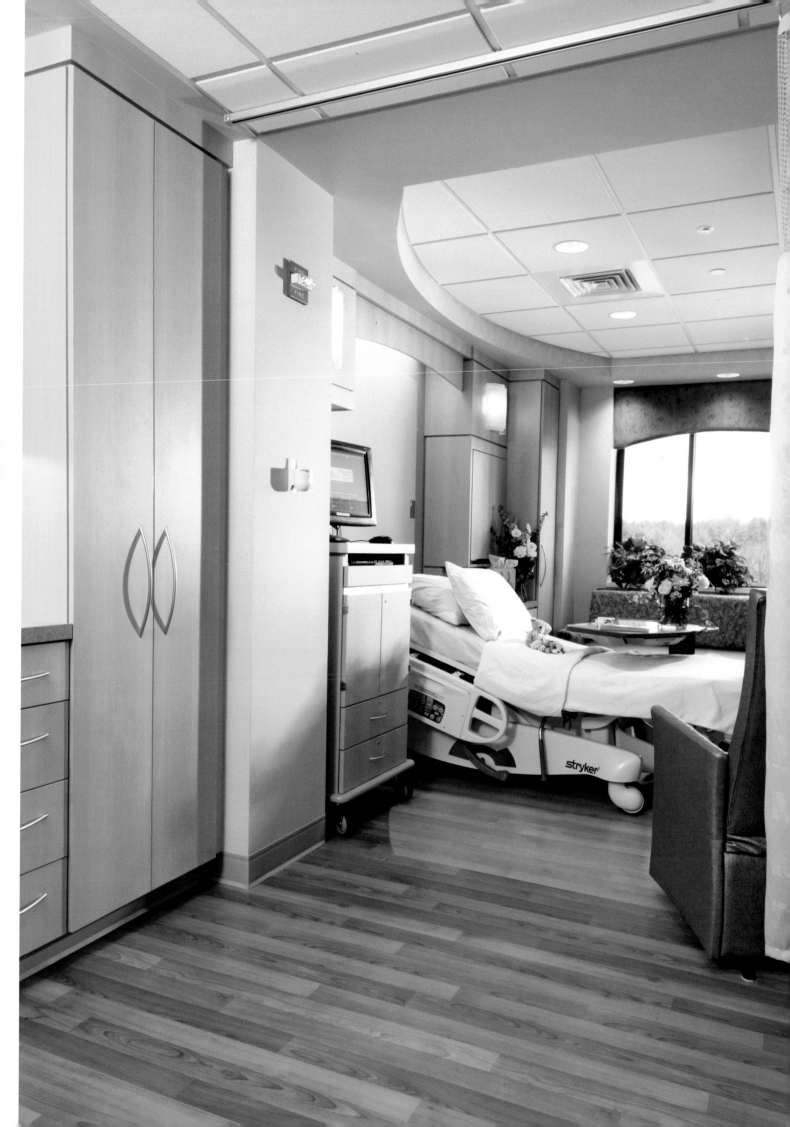

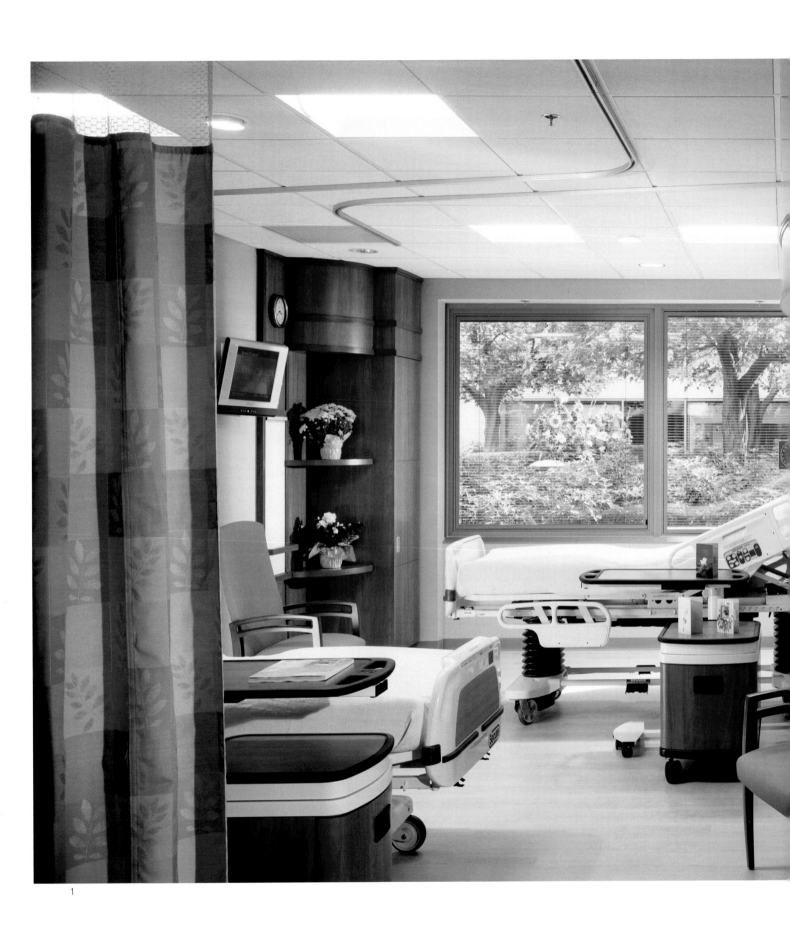

1

2

Beaumont South Tower Addition
Royal Oak, Michigan, USA
Harley Ellis Devereaux
1   Semi-private rooms offer a unique "foot-to-foot" layout and allows
    views and privacy to both patients, even with cubicle curtains drawn
Photography: Justin Maconochie Photography

Providence Newberg Medical Center
Newberg, Oregon, USA
Mahlum Architects
2   Rooms were designed to maximize an outward orientation for patients
    and visitors creating a sense of openness to the natural beauty of the
    outdoors and thus providing quality healing environments
Photography: Eckert & Eckert

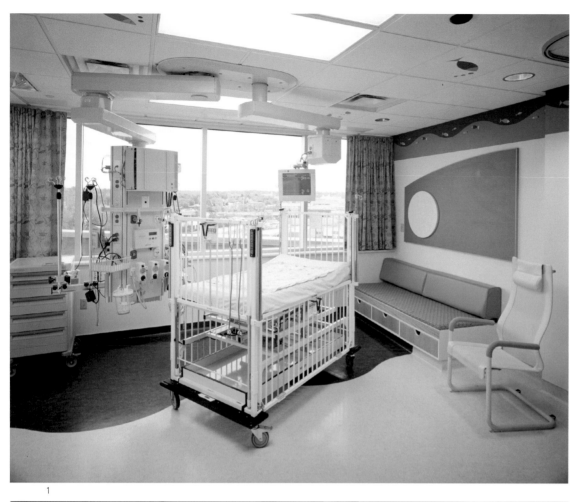

1

2

3

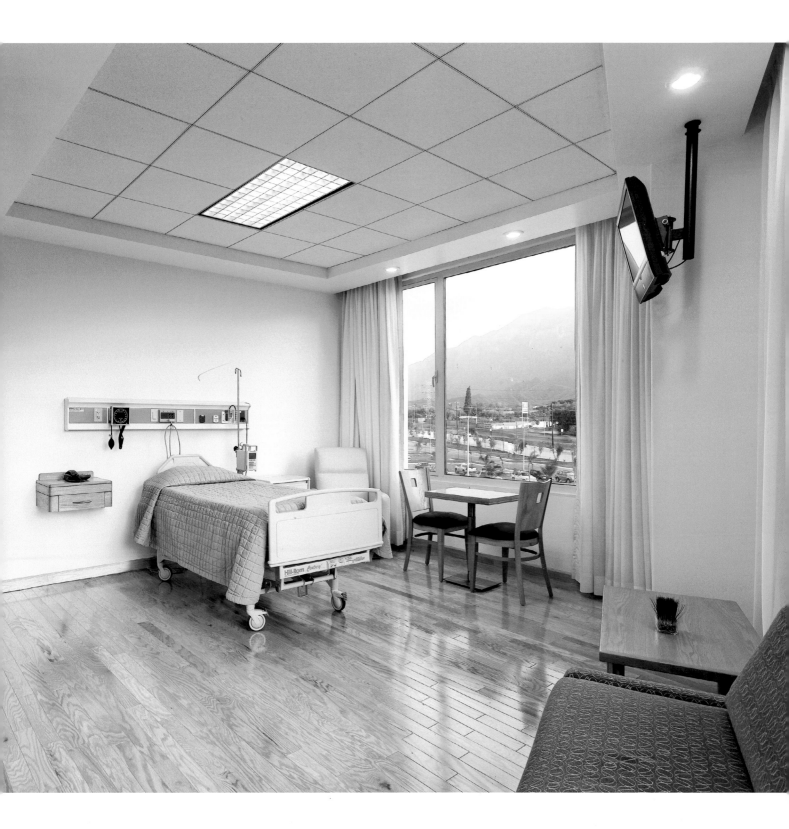

Children's Hospital
Omaha, Nebraska, USA
HDR Architecture, Inc.

1   Each pediatric-intensive-care room includes a suspended
    power column that houses all critical care needs and
    rotates around the patient, thereby offering the caregiver
    maximum flexibility with patients

2   All patient rooms are private and offer calming views of
    the natural landscape. A built-in parent sleeping bed, desk
    with computer port, private bath/shower, and refrigerator
    allow family to gather and stay as long as necessary.

Photography: Tom Kessler Photography

Christus Muguerza del Sur
Monterrey, Mexico
HKS Architects, Inc.

3   Larger patient rooms accommodate visiting family members
    and friends. The spectacular surrounding views aid the
    healing process.

Photography: Blake Marvin

Abbott Northwestern Heart Hospital
Minneapolis, Minnesota, USA
HKS Architects, Inc.

1   The family suites with dramatic views from the living area
    provide additional areas for longer stays
2   The acuity-adaptable patient rooms enabled with advance
    technology provide space for families and caregivers

Photography: Ed LaCasse

1

2

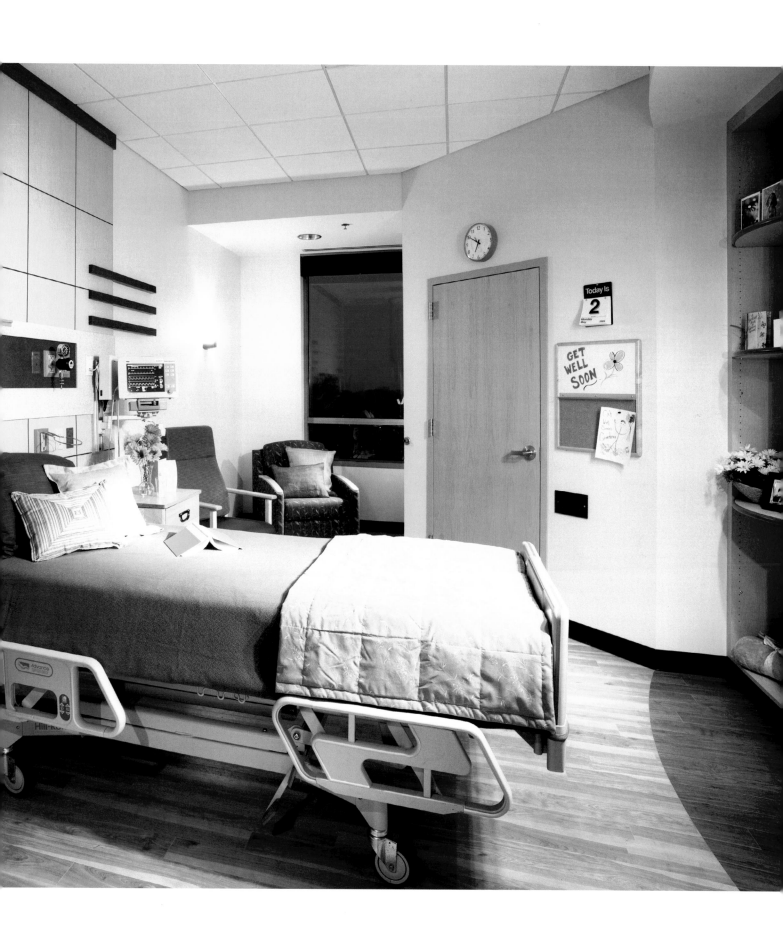

Clarian West Medical Center
Avon, Indiana, USA
HKS Architects, Inc.

1   Patient rooms provide floor-to-ceiling windows for patient
     views to the garden
2   The LDRPs include amenities such as a family sleep area,
     refrigerator, and a flat-panel plasma screen TV
Photography: Ed LaCasse

Washington Regional Medical Center
Fayetteville, Arkansas, USA
HKS Architects, Inc.

3   The LDRP, with inboard toilet, provides expansive views to
     the Arkansas countryside
Photography: Ed LaCasse

2

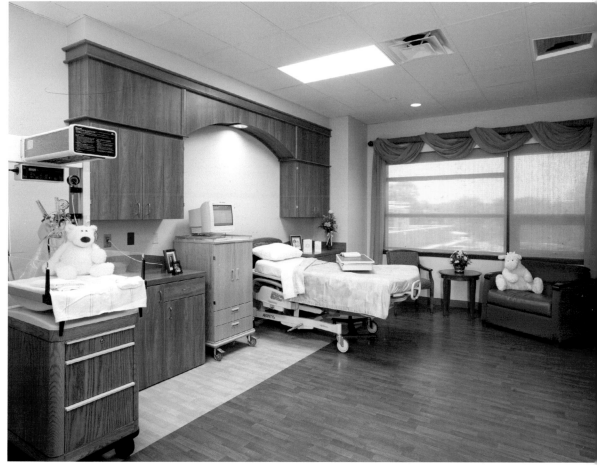

3

Clarian North Medical Center
Carmel, Indiana, USA
HKS Architects, Inc.

1   The universal medical/surgical patient room
    affords the patient and family privacy and
    comfort with access to the latest technology

Photography: Jeff Millies, Hedrich Blessing Photography

1

Parker Adventist Hospital
Parker, Colorado, USA
HKS Architects, Inc.

1   Calm colors such as mocha, buff, and tan feature in the interior of this patient room
2   Optimum patient and family comfort is ensured with large and spacious rooms
3   Additional details such as the contemporary-look chair and the design elements
    on the flooring make this room a pleasant space
Photography: Ed LaCasse

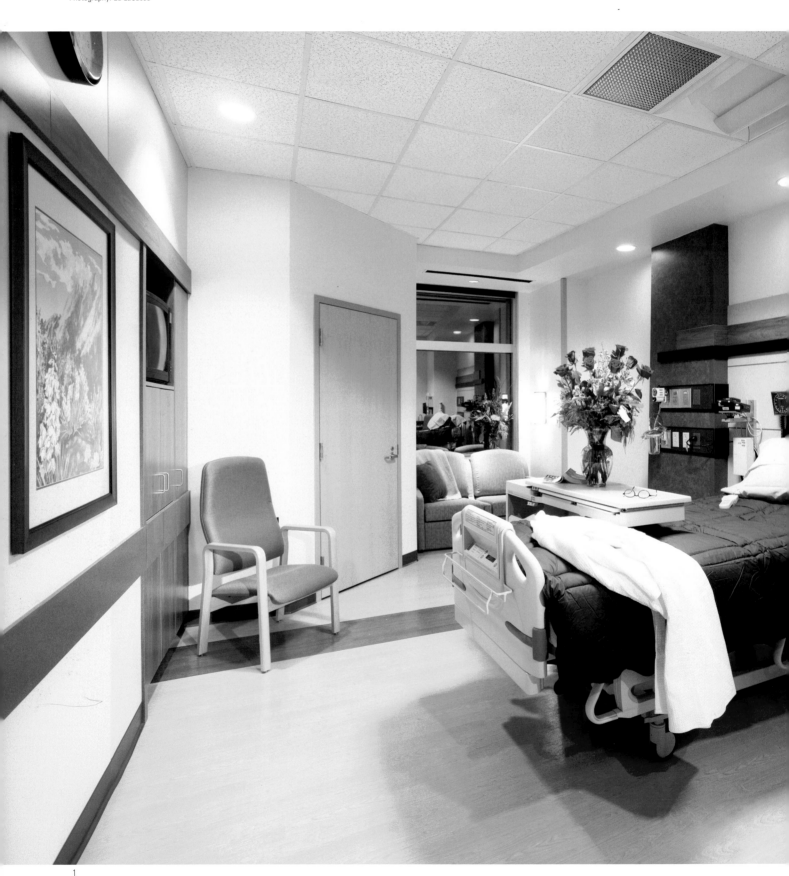

1

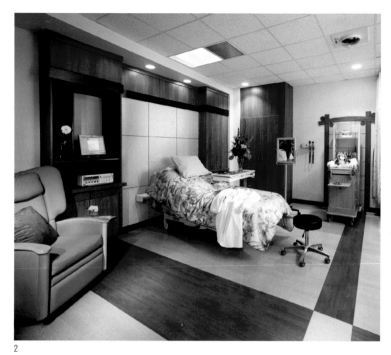

2

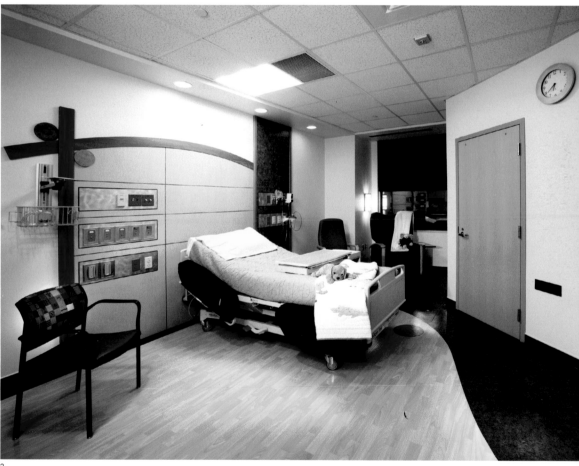

3

2

3

1

2

3

The Wisconsin Heart Hospital
Wauwatosa, Wisconsin, USA
HDR Architecture, Inc.

1   Wood, stone, and earth tones introduced in
     the lobby area are continued in the cafeteria
     to exude warmth and a totally relaxing
     atmosphere

Photography: Mark Ballogg

Sentara Heart Hospital
Norfolk, Virginia, USA
HDR Architecture, Inc.

2   The quaint dining café is just one of many
     public amenities on the first floor, which
     includes a lending library, conference center,
     children's play area, and gift shop

Photography: Mark Ballogg

Parker Adventist Hospital
Parker, Colorado, USA
HKS Architects, Inc.

3   The café area has elegant lighting and
     floors that impart a luxurious feel

Photography: Ed LaCasse

2

Clarian West Medical Center
Avon, Indiana, USA
HKS Architects, Inc.

1   The three-story atrium with a stone fireplace
    and outdoor views provides a restful and
    comfortable atmosphere for the garden café

Photography: Ed LaCasse

Providence Newberg Medical Center
Newberg, Oregon, USA
Mahlum Architects

2   Abundant natural light fills the two-story
    cafeteria. Views out to the healing garden
    and Parrett Mountain offer patients, visitors,
    and staff the opportunity to escape the
    stress of the inpatient setting.

Photography: Benjamin Benschneider

1

McKay-Dee Hospital Center
Ogden, Utah, USA
HKS Architects, Inc.
1   The food court feels more like a hospitality
    dining area than a hospital
Photography: Blake Marvin

Bloorview Kids Rehab
Toronto, Ontario, Canada
Montgomery Sisam Architects | Stantec Architecture
2   Generous glazing provides ample natural light and
    establishes a strong connection to the adjacent
    wooded ravine
Photography: Tom Arban Photography

Exeter Hospital
Exeter, New Hampshire, USA
JSA Inc.
3   Café dining area
Photography: Blind Dog Photography

Index

Abramson Teiger Architects — www.abramsonteiger.com
16, 143, 166

Harley Ellis Devereaux — www.harleyellis.com
14, 20, 88, 95, 164, 176, 188, 200

HDR Architecture, Inc. — www.hdrinc.com
21, 42, 72, 74, 92, 93, 114, 142, 144, 149, 184, 198, 202, 215, 216

HKS Architects, Inc. — www.hksinc.com
10, 22, 24, 26, 30, 32, 38, 46, 48, 50, 52, 56, 58, 62, 68, 75, 76, 77, 82, 85, 89, 90, 94, 100, 102, 106, 112, 116, 118,
122, 124, 126, 128, 132, 137, 138, 140, 146, 150, 152, 156, 158, 160, 161, 168, 170, 174, 180, 190, 192, 193, 194,
203, 204, 206, 207, 208, 210, 217, 218, 220

HMC Architects — www.hmcgroup.com
36, 37, 171

JSA Inc. — www.jsainc.com
84, 96, 112, 113, 126, 136, 177, 185, 199, 215, 221

Kirksey Architecture — www.kirksey.com
17, 28, 44, 78, 98, 130, 148, 214

Mahlum Architects — www.mahlum.com
18, 115, 167, 201, 219

Montgomery Sisam | Stantec Architecture — www.montgomerysisam.com   www.stantec.com
126, 221

Saunders + Wiant Architects — www.architectsoc.com
80, 86, 87, 92, 113, 120, 143, 166, 172, 178, 182, 186